# Are We Living *in the* End Times?

## BIBLICAL ANSWERS TO 7 QUESTIONS ABOUT THE FUTURE

# Dr. Robert Jeffress

DR. ROBERT JEFFRESS
Pathway
TO Victory

Praise for *Are We Living in the End Times?*

"My friend Dr. Robert Jeffress is one of the most influential evangelicals on the globe and, without a doubt, one of the most pro-Israel."

—Dr. Mike Evans, founder of the Friends of Zion Museum in Jerusalem

"Dr. Robert Jeffress is one of America's most loved and respected pastors. Always a fount of godly wisdom, strength, and encouragement on prophetic events. It's an honor to call him a friend."

—Sheila Walsh, Bible teacher and best-selling author, host of TBN's *Praise*

# Contents

Note from the Author ...................................................... 6

Introduction: Your Future Matters Today ......................... 8

1. What Does the Bible Mean by the End Times? ...... 16

2. What Role Does Israel Play in the End Times? ....... 35

3. What News Events Signal the End Times? ............. 56

4. What Are the Major Events of the End Times? ....... 69

5. What's the Difference between the Rapture and the Second Coming in the End Times? ........................ 85

6. Why Has God Delayed the End Times? ............... 104

7. How Do I Prepare for the End Times? ................. 112

Appendix A: The Rise of Radical Islam ......................... 132

Appendix B: More Answers about the End Times ......... 150

Notes ................................................................... 199

About Dr. Robert Jeffress ............................................ 206

About *Pathway to Victory* ............................................. 208

# Note from the Author

"Are we living in the end times?"

"What is the next event on God's prophetic timeline?"

"Do the current world events indicate that Jesus is coming soon?"

For years, I've heard questions like these from men and women in the church I pastor and from those who watch or listen to *Pathway to Victory*. But in light of increasing global catastrophes—such as the COVID-19 pandemic, devastating natural disasters, and escalating wars and violence around the world, including the 2022 Russian invasion of Ukraine and the 2023 attack on Israel by the terrorist organization Hamas—people have been asking about the end times with increased urgency. In fact, a recent Pew Research survey showed that almost 40 percent of Americans believe that the world is going to end soon.[1] And at least one-third of Americans admit to doomsday prepping—buying supplies to prepare for the end of the world—having spent a staggering $11 billion on survival items in just one year.[2]

Maybe you are concerned about current events

and wondering about the end times too. Perhaps you've heard conflicting teachings about end-times prophecy, or maybe you have received no teaching at all. Or possibly you have become disillusioned by false predictions of the end of the world.

The good news is that end-times prophecy does not need to be complicated or confusing. In this book, I will provide biblical answers to common questions about the end times. Not only that, but I will show you why understanding biblical prophecy is critical to your life today, as well as to your future.

In *Are We Living in the End Times?* you will find clear, relevant teaching directly from the Bible that reveals God's will for you and the entire world. I pray that God will use these answers to fill you with peace, joy, and excitement as we look forward to our Lord's certain return.

Anticipating His coming kingdom,

Dr. Robert Jeffress
Senior Pastor, First Baptist Church,
Dallas, Texas
Bible Teacher, *Pathway to Victory*

# Introduction
# Your Future Matters Today

It feels as if the world is spinning out of control, doesn't it? Every day, we are bombarded with disturbing headlines. Violent crime is on the rise, and conflicts are flaring up across the globe, with terrorists and dictators using unprecedented technologies. Economies are increasingly unstable, virus strains are causing panic, and natural disasters are wreaking havoc all over the earth. And complicating all these matters is the growing divisiveness in our nation and the growing distrust of our broken government and biased media.

If you're concerned about events unfolding around the world, you're not alone. According to one news source, "US officials say this confluence of crises poses epic concern and historic danger."[1] Even seasoned former defense secretary Bob Gates recently admitted, "America is facing the most crises since World War II ended."[2] It certainly seems like things couldn't get much worse!

Many Christians are wondering if we are seeing biblical prophecy being fulfilled in our lifetimes. In

Luke 21:10–11, Jesus gave His disciples a glimpse of what the world will be like during the end times: "Nation will rise against nation and kingdom against kingdom, and there will be great earthquakes, and in various places plagues and famines; and there will be terrors and great signs from heaven."

As if that weren't dire enough, look at the apostle Paul's description of the last days: "In the last days difficult times will come. For men will be lovers of self, lovers of money, boastful, arrogant, revilers, disobedient to parents, ungrateful, unholy, unloving, irreconcilable, malicious gossips, without self-control, brutal, haters of good, treacherous, reckless, conceited, lovers of pleasure rather than lovers of God, holding to a form of godliness, although they have denied its power" (2 Timothy 3:1–5). When we read these descriptions in Scripture and compare them with current events, it's natural for Christians to wonder, "Are we living in the end times?"

Thankfully, Scripture answers this question and gives Christians great hope for the future. In this book, I will share biblical answers to these pressing questions about the end times:

- What does the Bible mean by the end times?
- What role does Israel play in the end times?

- What news events signal the end times?

- What are the major events of the end times?

- What's the difference between the rapture and the second coming in the end times?

- Why has God delayed the end times?

- How do I prepare for the end times?

Now, I realize that many Christians get confused when we start talking about the end times. The fact is, you can be very smart and still get tangled up in some of the details of Bible prophecy. Before we look at what the Bible says about specific events God has planned for the end times, let's first consider the question: Why should we study the subject of Bible prophecy?

## Why Study Bible Prophecy?

Many people think Bible prophecy is not relevant today. They prefer to talk about topics like how to improve your marriage or how to have a better prayer life. They say those are the things Christians should be studying and discussing, not the end times.

Let me share three reasons it is important for Christians to understand Bible prophecy.

## Prophecy Is a Major Theme of the Bible

One way to know what is important to God is to know what subjects are covered the most in His Word. And prophecy is a major theme of the Bible. For example, did you know there are eighteen hundred references in the Bible to the second coming of Christ? In the New Testament, 1 in every 30 verses has to do with the return of Jesus Christ. In fact, 23 of the 27 books of the New Testament deal with the subject of Christ's return. And in the Old Testament, for every prophecy about the first coming of the Messiah to Bethlehem, there are 8 verses about the second coming of Christ. Clearly, the return of Jesus Christ is a major theme in the Bible, which is why we need to understand it.

## Prophecy Helps Us Interpret and Apply the Bible

Studying Bible prophecy also helps us interpret and apply the Bible accurately. You can't fully understand the Old Testament prophets, Jesus's parables and teachings, or the epistles without understanding prophecy. Prophecy is the framework on which we hang the rest of the Bible.

Let's look at two illustrations of that, one from the Old Testament and one from the New Testament. The first example is Isaiah 65:20: "No longer will there be in it an infant who lives but a few days, or an old man who does not live out his days; for the youth will die at the age of one hundred and the one who does not reach the age of one hundred will be thought accursed." Isaiah was describing a time when infants don't die, and people live one hundred years. What time was Isaiah talking about? He obviously wasn't talking about now. Even with our advances in medicine, babies still die, and few people reach the age of one hundred. Was Isaiah talking about heaven? No, Revelation 21:4 says there is no death in heaven. So what time was Isaiah talking about? He was talking about a future period called the millennium when Jesus will reign on earth for a thousand years. During that time, the curse of sin will be partially removed. You can't understand that without knowing Bible prophecy.

The second example is Matthew 25:35–40. Jesus said, "'I was hungry, and you gave Me something to eat; I was thirsty, and you gave Me something to drink; I was a stranger, and you invited Me in; naked, and you clothed Me; I was sick, and you visited Me; I was in prison, and you came to Me.' Then the righteous will answer Him, 'Lord, when did we see You hungry, and feed You, or thirsty, and give You something to drink? And when did we see You a stranger, and invite You in, or naked, and clothe You? When did we see You sick, or in prison, and come to You?' The King will answer and say to them, 'Truly I say to you, to the extent that you did it to one of these brothers of Mine, even the least of them, you did it to Me.'"

I once heard somebody say, "I'm a Matthew 25 Christian. My faith is centered on taking care of the least of these." Now, we should be merciful to those in need. That's certainly the evidence of being a Christian. But is doing good things for the least of these the core of the Christian faith? Is that what the apostles proclaimed and gave their lives for? No, the heart of Christianity is repentance from sin and the forgiveness of God through Jesus Christ. As Peter preached in Acts 2:38, "Repent, and each of you be baptized in the name of Jesus Christ for the forgiveness of your sins."

If repentance and faith are the core of Christianity, then what was Jesus talking about in Matthew 25? He was teaching about the end times. In Matthew 24:3, the disciples asked Jesus, "What will be the sign of Your coming, and of the end of the age?" Jesus answered this question by giving them a timeline of Bible prophecy. In Matthew 25:35–40, Jesus was referring to the 144,000 Jewish witnesses who will be saved during the tribulation. Although those witnesses will be protected by God, they will suffer, be imprisoned, and be denied food and drink. Jesus was saying to that future age, "To the extent that you minister to one of these witnesses of Mine, it is a sign of your love for Me. When you feed them, clothe them, and take them in, it is as if you are doing the same thing to Me."

You can't understand this teaching of Jesus if you don't understand how it fits into Bible prophecy. Prophecy is the key to interpreting and applying the Bible correctly.

## Prophecy Motivates Us toward Godly Living

Understanding Bible prophecy also motivates us toward godly living. The reason God tells us about the end times is not to satisfy our curiosity; it is to increase our obedience to Him.

One of the consistent themes of the Bible is that life as we know it is coming to an end. Whether that end will come through death or the return of the Lord Jesus Christ, Scripture is clear that soon and very soon, our lives are about to undergo a big change. And realizing that everything around us is coming to an end ought to motivate us to live godly lives.

Revelation 22:7 says, "Behold, I am coming quickly. Blessed is he who heeds the words of the prophecy of this book." The fact that Jesus is coming back and this world is coming to an end is a powerful incentive for us to obey God consistently and completely. That's why we study Bible prophecy, and that's why I've written this book. My prayer for you is that by understanding God's plan for the end times, you will be motivated to live a godly life and share the gospel with as many people as possible while there is still time.

Come soon, Lord Jesus!

# 1

# What Does the Bible Mean by the End Times?

I have discovered that the subject of the end times brings various reactions from different people. The first time I found that out, I learned it the hard way.

I was a sophomore at Richardson High School, and our English teacher gave us an assignment to present, as creatively as possible, a book report on any book of our choosing. Well, about that time, Hal Lindsey's book *The Late Great Planet Earth* had just come out.[1] So I thought, *I'll present my book report on* The Late Great Planet Earth, *and I'll do it as creatively as possible.*

When the day came to give my book report, I spent the first twenty minutes of my presentation discussing the various things Lindsey talked about, giving special attention to the invasion of Israel by the forces from the north, which Lindsey identified as Russia. I thought the subject would be of particular interest because at that very time, President Nixon was in Moscow trying to ease the Soviet–U.S. tension.

Now what the class didn't know was that I had arranged, at just the right time, for the assistant principal to come over the PA system with a fake announcement. And just right on cue as soon as I was wrapping up, the little *ding, ding, ding* came on over the PA system, and the assistant principal, piping into our room, gave the fake announcement I had planned. He said, "We have just received word from the United Press International that Russia has invaded Israel. President Nixon is on his way back to Washington, DC, on Air Force One. Students and faculty members are urged to leave immediately and seek shelter."

My teacher yelled, "It's true!" As the students in my classroom started heading toward the exit, I calmed everybody down. I explained, "This was just an illustration of how current events can coincide with Bible prophecy."

Now, that would have been okay; however, the assistant principal made a mistake. Instead of piping that fake announcement only into our classroom, the announcement went to the entire school. All of a sudden, I started hearing lockers slamming upstairs, with students running and yelling. Everybody headed toward the exits that day! Decades later, I still have classmates who were there that spring day who remind me and kid me about the day everybody thought the world was coming to an end.

Unfortunately, I didn't get an A on the project. But it reminds us of the truth that there is going to come a time, the Bible says, when the world is going to be filled with all kinds of calamities. There will be a time of tribulation, economic collapse, crisis, and catastrophe. Many people today are wondering, "Do the events around us indicate that the end is drawing near?"

I agree that today's news is filled with calamities, but as Christians, we have nothing to worry about. I can assure you that we are not yet in the end times, because the Bible says one other event must happen first. This is good news for us. No one who believes in Christ today will have to endure any part of the end-times tribulation because of one pivotal event: the rapture of the church.

The rapture is the next event on God's prophetic timeline, in which Jesus will snatch away all believers to be with Him in heaven before the tribulation begins. The rapture will include every person who has put their faith in Jesus Christ. This is our great hope! (I'll talk more about this event in chapter 5.)

Before we dive into what the Bible says about the

end times, let's take a brief historical perspective on end-times expectations. Knowing history can prevent us from making critical mistakes about trying to predict when the end times will take place.

# The "End of the World" throughout History

Ever since Jesus Christ ascended to heaven, Christians have believed He would return someday. However, Jesus said, "Of that day and hour no one knows, not even the angels of heaven, nor the Son, but the Father alone" (Matthew 24:36). When Jesus walked the earth, even He didn't know the exact day and time that He would return. How foolish we would be to think we know more than Jesus!

Unfortunately, that warning from our Lord has not stopped believers over the centuries from trying to predict the date for the return of Jesus Christ:

- In AD 160, Montanus said the new Jerusalem was about to descend from heaven to a field in Asia Minor (modern-day Turkey). Many Christians believed him and waited on the plain on the day Montanus stated. They were very disappointed.[2]

- As the year AD 1000 approached, many clerics predicted that Jesus was about to return. The appearance of Halley's comet in 989, as well as other disasters and astronomical events, added to the expectation that the end was near.[3]

- A few hundred years later, Pope Innocent III believed that if you added 666 ("the number of the beast" in Revelation 13:18) to the date he believed Islam was founded, you would get the date Jesus would return. The pope came up with the year 1284.[4]

- Christopher Columbus wrote *The Book of Prophecies*, which listed events he thought must take place before Christ's return. He calculated that the world would end in 1656 or 1658.[5]

- In 1831, William Miller, the founder of the Adventist movement, predicted Jesus would return on March 21, 1844. When that day came and went, Miller said the date of Christ's return was actually October 22, 1844. When that date yielded no Jesus either, it was dubbed by newspapers as "the Great Disappointment."[6]

- Charles Taze Russell, the founder of the Jehovah's Witnesses, predicted that Jesus would return in 1914. Russell went on to predict seven other dates the world would end, which all came and went.[7]

- Christian radio broadcaster Harold Camping made as many as thirteen failed predictions of when Christ would return, the last one being October 21, 2011.[8] His ministry spent more than $100 million publicizing his erroneous proclamations! Many people gave Camping their entire life savings, and several injuries and at least one death resulted from the panic his predictions caused.[9]

These are only a handful of the countless end-times predictions made over the centuries.

Looking at this list, you may think that only Christians and cults have been making predictions about the end of the world. However, many non-Christians, using scientific-sounding terminology, have made terrifying doomsday predictions as well. In 1967, a best-selling book predicted mass starvation would take place in the developing world by 1975.[10] When 1975 rolled around without mass starvation, many scientists moved on to the next catastrophe and predicted that global cooling would send us into a new ice age by the year 2000.[11] United Nations official Noel Brown said that entire nations would be under water from melting ice if global warming was not reversed by 2000.[12] Former vice president Al Gore said that we only had until 2016 before we reached the point of no return.[13] And congresswoman Alexandria Ocasio-Cortez said that we only have until the year 2031 to empower the government to take control of all industry in order to eliminate carbon emissions.[14] And though 2031 is still many years in the future, I suspect her prediction will yield the same results as every other doomsday prediction.

## Rules for End-Times Study

So, as Christians, what are we to make of all these failed predictions? To understand the signs of the times, we need to learn three important lessons from history and from Scripture.

First of all, we must not be alarmed by doomsday predictions regarding the environment. In Genesis 8:21, after God destroyed the world with a flood, He made a promise to Noah and his family: "I will never again curse the ground on account of man, for the intent of man's heart is evil from his youth; and I will never again destroy every living thing, as I have done." Did you catch that? God promised to never again destroy the earth with a flood. In verse 22, He continued, "While the earth remains, seedtime and harvest, and cold and heat, and summer and winter, and day and night shall not cease."

Because of God's promise, we know that the seasons will continue—both cold and heat—for as long as the earth endures, and that civilization will never again be destroyed by a flood. Thus, we need not fear excessive global warming or rising sea levels. God sealed His covenant with Noah with the sign of the rainbow, confirming that sea levels will never again destroy civilization (9:12–15). Knowing God's Word calms our fears and prevents us from being deceived by doomsday climate alarmists.

Second, we would do well to learn from history and stay away from trying to predict the exact date of any end-times event. In Matthew 24:36–39, Jesus said, "Of that day and hour no one knows, not even the angels of heaven, nor the Son, but the Father alone. For the coming of the Son of Man will be just like the days of Noah. For as in those days before the flood they were eating and drinking, marrying and giving in marriage, until the day that Noah entered the ark, and they did not understand until the flood came and took them all away; so will the coming of the Son of Man be." To repeat, we must keep in mind that if Jesus did not know the day and hour of His return, then we would be arrogant to think that we could figure it out.

This brings up a third error we should also avoid. Just because we cannot know the exact time or date that Christ is coming back doesn't mean we should ignore the subject of the end times altogether. Some Christians do, but they shouldn't. Look at the conclusion Jesus drew from the fact that no one but the Father knows when He will return: "Therefore be on the alert, for you do not know which day your Lord is coming. But be sure of this, that if the head of the house had known at what time of the night the thief was coming, he would have been on the alert and would not have allowed his house to be broken into. For this reason you also must be ready; for the Son of Man is coming at an hour when you do not think He will" (vv. 42–44).

The fact that we cannot know exactly when Christ will return means that we must be ready at all times. Just a few verses earlier, in Matthew 24:32–35, Jesus said, "Learn the parable from the fig tree: when its branch has already become tender and puts forth its leaves, you know that summer is near; so, you too, when you see all these things, recognize that He is near, right at the door. Truly I say to you, this generation will not pass away until all these things take place. Heaven and earth will pass away, but My words will not pass away."

Although we cannot know the exact date or time of His return, Jesus commanded us to observe the signs of the end times and to act accordingly.

# Labor Pains

So, what are the signs of the end times? And how can we learn the lesson of the fig tree and be alert in a way that honors Jesus? To help you understand this, let me use an analogy Jesus used earlier in this same passage to describe the state of our world: the analogy of pregnancy.

When a woman becomes pregnant, the gestation lasts for forty weeks (just over nine months). Now, when my daughter Julia was pregnant with her triplets, the babies came early. In pregnancies with multiple children, they almost always do. However, even single babies can come a week or two before or after their due date. In fact, only one in twenty-five babies is born on the exact due date. Nine months is just an estimate.[15] But parents know the rough time period that the child should arrive. As the day approaches, the signs of the baby's impending delivery become more apparent. Aside from the mother's growing belly, she can feel the baby move inside her, her contractions increase, and then suddenly she goes into labor.

Jesus used the same analogy for His second coming. In Matthew 24:3, the disciples asked Jesus, "What will be the sign of Your coming, and of the end of the age?" Beginning in Matthew 24:4, Jesus answered the disciples' question: "See to it that no one misleads you. For many will come in My name, saying, 'I am the Christ,' and will mislead many. You will be hearing of wars and rumors of wars. See that you are not frightened, for those things must take place, but that is not yet the end. For nation will rise against nation, and kingdom against kingdom, and in various places there will be famines and earthquakes. But all these things are merely the beginning of birth pangs" (vv. 4–8).

Jesus explained that the end of the age will be like a woman going into labor. Spiritual deception, wars, famines, and earthquakes are all just contractions indicating that this age is winding down, and that Christ's kingdom will soon arrive.

About twenty years after Jesus gave this warning to His disciples, the apostle Paul used the same analogy of labor pains to describe the Lord's return. In 1 Thessalonians 5:1–3, he wrote, "Now as to the times and the epochs, brethren, you have no need of anything to be written to you. For you yourselves know full well that the day of the Lord will come just like a thief in the night. While they are saying, 'Peace and safety!' then destruction will come upon them suddenly like labor pains upon a woman with child, and they will not escape." As the time for Christ's return approaches, the signs will increase and increase until suddenly, the world will go into labor.

Now, let's look at another aspect of the birth analogy to understand the next event on God's prophetic timeline: the rapture of the church. As I mentioned earlier, the Bible teaches that at the rapture, Jesus will suddenly appear, and all Christians on earth will be "caught up . . . in the clouds to meet the Lord in the air" (1 Thessalonians 4:17) before the end times begin.

What does the rapture have to do with the analogy of birth? In most pregnancies, a woman's water breaks after she has gone into labor. But sometimes this happens before the labor begins. When this occurs, the child will inevitably come within one to seven days.[16]

The rapture of the church will be like the rupture of a woman's water before labor. This event will lead to a time the Bible calls the tribulation, and then Christ will return to earth at the end of the seven-year tribulation. As we have seen, the rapture is the next event on God's prophetic timeline. But is it about to happen? To continue the analogy, are we about nine months along in the pregnancy? Are the signs of Christ's return—the "labor pains"—increasing? Are we living in the end times?

# Last Days and End Times

I do believe we are living in a period of time the Bible calls the "last days." Although no one knows exactly where we are on God's prophetic clock, we do know that the countdown to Christ's return has begun.

Let me explain what I mean by the terms *last days* and *end times*.

## Last Days

In one sense, the countdown to the end times began when Jesus ascended into heaven. That is when the clock started ticking down toward the date of Jesus's second coming. So in that sense, we are living in the "last days" as we await Christ's return:

> In these *last days* [God] has spoken to us in His Son, whom He appointed heir of all things, through whom also He made the world. (Hebrews 1:2)

For He was foreknown before the foundation of the world, but has appeared in these *last times* for the sake of you who through Him are believers in God, who raised Him from the dead and gave Him glory, so that your faith and hope are in God. (1 Peter 1:20–21)

These men are not drunk, as you suppose, for it is only the third hour of the day; but this is what was spoken of through the prophet Joel:

> "And it shall be in the *last days*," God says,
>
> "That I will pour forth of My Spirit on all mankind;
>
> And your sons and your daughters shall prophesy,
>
> And your young men shall see visions,
>
> And your old men shall dream dreams;
>
> Even on My bondslaves, both men and women,
>
> I will in those days pour forth of My Spirit
>
> And they shall prophesy." (Acts 2:15–18)

Thus, the term *last days* in the Bible roughly equates to the church age, which began on the day of Pentecost. In Romans 11:2–5, Paul explained that during this time, the Jews have hardened their hearts toward the gospel, and God has opened salvation to Gentiles (non-Jews). The church age will end with the rapture when Jesus takes the church to be with Him in heaven.

## End Times

When I use the term *end times*, I am referring to the specific events that will begin with the rapture of the church. Immediately after the rapture has occurred, the final seven years of earth's history—a period the Bible calls the tribulation—will begin. This is the time period when a world dictator called the Antichrist will rule the earth. Halfway through those seven years, this ruler will betray Israel and instigate a period of unparalleled persecution for the final three and a half years, called the "great tribulation" (Matthew 24:21). The climax of the great tribulation will be a world confrontation called Armageddon, which will end with Jesus Christ visibly appearing in the sky, defeating His enemies, and establishing His thousand-year kingdom in Jerusalem.

When I talk about the *end times* in this book, I am

specifically talking about the seven years of tribulation that will begin with the rapture of the church and will conclude with Christ's visible second coming seven years later.

# The Last of the Last Days

So, as I define it here, we are not yet living in the end times, because the rapture has not yet happened. However, I am convinced that we are living in what the Bible calls the "last days." And as I look at some of the current news events around the world, I believe that we are in the last of the last days. Jesus Christ could suddenly appear at any moment to rapture His church and usher in the end-times tribulation.

Even since before Jesus's ascension into heaven, believers have come to expect that He might establish His kingdom within their lifetimes. Theologians call this the doctrine of imminence. In fact, the disciples, just before Jesus's ascension, asked, "Lord, is it at this time You are restoring the kingdom to Israel?" (Acts 1:6). Jesus's answer was clear: "It is not for you to know times or epochs which the Father has fixed by His own authority" (v. 7). Rather, Jesus went on to explain that the disciples have a job to do: to be worldwide witnesses of the death and resurrection of Jesus Christ through the power of the Holy Spirit (v. 8). Our job isn't to set dates, but to share the gospel with as many people as we can so they might be prepared for when Christ raptures His church and brings about the end-times tribulation described in biblical prophecy. To help ourselves and others prepare for this once-in-a-lifetime event, we must keep two principles in mind.

First, the signs of the end times—including international conflict, persecution of believers, and apostasy—are present in every generation. Ever since the fall of mankind, the world has been ravaged by wars, plagues, natural disasters, spiritual deception, and economic chaos. Human evil and suffering go back as far as Adam and Eve's fall in Genesis 3. That's why it is a mistake to take any single headline and say, "This means the end is here!" Instead, we need to look at the general direction of the way events are moving to determine what is happening.

Second, the signs of the times will accelerate in intensity and frequency as we approach the end. Jesus said, "All these things are merely the beginning of birth pangs" (Matthew 24:8). Remember Jesus's analogy of an expectant mother? A pregnant woman can look at the calendar and have a general idea of when her baby is coming. As the day approaches, she begins to experience labor pains—a sign that something big is about to happen. Sometimes labor pains start and then subside. But then comes a time when those labor pains increase in frequency and intensity, and she knows the baby is coming. We need to see if the contractions are moving closer together, so to speak.

If we were to plot these signs of the times—these "contractions"—on a graph that started when Christ ascended into heaven (Acts 1:9), we would see that during the last two thousand years, the graph would go up and down. The signs of the times have increased and then decreased through the centuries. But Jesus said as we get closer to the end, the graph will move up. For two thousand years, we have seen the signs of the end times come and go, but we are starting to see that graph continually go up as the end approaches, signaling that our present age is coming to a close and that the rapture is just around the corner.[17]

Although the physical condition of many people around the world has never been better, the spiritual condition of the human race overall has never been worse. We are more selfish than ever before. In addition, technology has made it so that a one-world government could easily be established. With communication satellites, the internet, and microchip technology, establishing a worldwide tyranny would not be difficult, especially if the world is in a panic from an event such as the rapture.

Thankfully, as I mentioned earlier, God has promised to spare believers in the current age from His wrath by rapturing us before the tribulation begins. Romans 8:1 says, "There is now no condemnation for those who are in Christ Jesus." We do not have to fear experiencing the wrath of God in the future, because God already took all the wrath that you and I deserve and poured it out on His Son as He hung on the cross two thousand years ago.[18] What great comfort this biblical truth gives all Christians during these uncertain times![19]

# 2

# What Role Does Israel Play in the End Times?

On October 7, 2023, the ruling regime in Gaza, Hamas, pulled off a surprise assault on Israel. In the early morning hours, Hamas rapidly shot thousands of rockets to overwhelm Israel's Iron Dome missile defense system and hit populated areas. Their fighters also flooded over the border, indiscriminately killing innocent civilians and taking hostages. Hundreds of people in Israel were murdered and thousands more were wounded and traumatized.

This kind of conflict in Israel has a very personal resonance with me. I was at the White House when then-President Trump announced the historic Abraham Accords, and later when these documents were signed. I was also invited to pray at the opening of the US embassy in Jerusalem, a world-historic event that took place five years ago. I believe the Abraham Accords and the embassy were key milestones of political, moral, and biblical significance.

Although the timing and the scale of the October 7 attack was a surprise, attacks against Israel have been ongoing for millennia. When we look at the persecution and suffering of the Jewish people throughout history, we realize that this is ultimately not a human struggle. It is a spiritual struggle against the forces of darkness.

You see, God said, "I'm going to create a people, the Jewish people, and they're going to be a human object lesson of a divine truth. It's through Israel that I'm going to display My power. It is through Israel that I'm going to display My lovingkindness. It is through Israel that I'm going to display My sovereignty, and I'm going to make this promise because they are My people: they will endure forever."

Did you know that Israel is the only nation in the world that has God's promise of endurance? God hasn't given that promise to the United States. America is not going to endure forever; we are going to fall at some point. That doesn't mean we become lackadaisical, and it doesn't mean we don't push back, but eventually America is going to fall. Only Israel, believing Israel, has the promise from God of endurance.

The reason Satan has his sights set on Israel is that if he can destroy Israel, then he can prove that

God is incapable of keeping His promises. From the very beginning, Satan has done everything he can to annihilate Israel. He's done it through human leaders like Pharaoh, Antiochus Epiphanes, Herod, and ultimately, the Antichrist. The Antichrist is the future world leader who will unleash the greatest persecution Israel has ever known, but the Antichrist will not succeed because Jesus Christ is going to return, and He will have the final say in Israel.

Someday, believing Israel will receive all the promises God has for her. But right now, what we're witnessing through the ongoing conflicts in Israel is a spiritual evil. It is Satan himself who is empowering terrorist groups and nations to try to wipe Israel from the land, but they will not succeed in their effort. That's the promise of God.

We need to recognize the spiritual war that is being waged against God's people in the nation of Israel. As Christians, we stand with the nation of Israel, and we condemn the evil, violent attacks on God's chosen people.

Most of the attacks we've seen throughout Israel's history are rooted in opposing claims over Israel's land, claims built on a false theology and a false history. You can read any history book or just pick up a Bible and see—Israel is not a usurper of the land they have.

They are the most well-documented group of native inhabitants ever to have occupied a piece of territory. Genesis 15:18–21 shows that God gave them the land they are now defending, dating all the way back to Abraham.

For thousands of years, God has attempted to bring the nation of Israel into a right relationship with Himself. Although there are many instances in the Old Testament of non-Jews (Gentiles) being saved, Genesis 11 shows the primary focus was on Israel.

# God's Call to Abraham

We are first introduced to Abraham, whom God chose to become the father of the nation of Israel, at the end of Genesis 11: "Terah lived seventy years, and became the father of Abram, Nahor and Haran" (v. 26). So Terah was the father of Abram (who later became known as Abraham, so I'll call him Abraham in this book).

## The Setting

Let's look at the setting of God's call to Abraham. The setting for this story is the city of Ur. At that time, Ur was a metropolitan city, something like New York or London today. It was a port city in Mesopotamia on the Persian Gulf, bordered by the Euphrates River.

One weekend when I was in college, I traveled to Austin to visit my girlfriend (who is now my wife), Amy, who was a student at the University of Texas. The university had a display of artifacts found in an excavation of Ur of the Chaldeans. We went to the exhibition, and it was amazing to see the things that had been discovered in this ancient city. It was a very advanced civilization.

The most important thing to know about Ur of the Chaldeans is that it was a center for idolatry. The descendants of Ham, one of Noah's sons, had settled in Ur, and they brought with them their idolatry. Although we would like to think Abraham's family differed from the pagans who lived around them, we find from reading Joshua 24:2–3 that Terah, Abraham's father, was a maker of idols. And not only that, but Abraham himself also was a worshiper of idols.

This is a key point: God did not look down at Abraham and say, "Abraham, because you're different from all the other people, because you worship Me instead of worshiping pagan gods, I'm going to call you for My purpose." No, it wasn't because of Abraham's righteousness that God called him; it was in spite of his unrighteousness that God called him.

May I pause for an important reminder? If you are a Christian, don't think it's because of anything good in you that God saved you. God didn't choose to save you because He looked at you and saw some spark of divinity or because you did good deeds that made you worth saving. Titus 3:5 says, "[God] saved us, not on the basis of deeds which we have done in righteousness, but according to His mercy." Our salvation is based solely on God's grace. By the way, if you are not yet a Christian, but you understand your sin and your need for a Savior and know that Jesus offers the gift of salvation, you didn't come to that understanding on your own. God has given you that understanding so that you might receive His undeserved gift of grace.

## The Command

God, out of His mercy, chose to save Abraham and gave this command in Genesis 12:1: "Go forth from your country and from your relatives and from your father's house to the land that I will show you." God was saying to Abraham, "I want you to uproot everything you have—your family, your possessions—and I want you to move to a distant land that I will eventually show you. You're to get up and start moving."

Think what that must have been like for Abraham to leave everyone and everything familiar to him and go to this unnamed country. Perhaps you know what

I'm talking about. God has given you a command. He's told you clearly what He wants you to do—it may not make any sense, but God has spoken. Remember, when God gives a command, that command doesn't always make sense, but it is always accompanied by a promise. I'll talk more about the promises God makes to us later. But first, let's look at God's promise to Abraham.

## God's Covenant with Abraham

In Genesis 12:2–3, we find God's promise to Abraham that followed His command:

> And I will make you a great nation,
>
> And I will bless you,
>
> And make your name great;
>
> And so you shall be a blessing;
>
> And I will bless those who bless you,
>
> And the one who curses you I will curse.
>
> And in you all the families of the earth will
> be blessed.

Let's look at the three components of the Abrahamic covenant.

41

**God Promised a Land**

God said to Abraham, in essence, "I will give you a land that will belong to you and your descendants forever." That was the first part of the Abrahamic covenant: the promise of a land. God promised to give Abraham and his descendants "the land which I will show you" (v. 1). He wasn't talking about heaven; He was talking about a land here on earth.

In Genesis 15:18–21 and Ezekiel 47:13–21, we find the specific boundaries of the land that belongs to Abraham's descendants. Interestingly, these passages describe land that Israel has not yet completely inhabited. The modern nation of Israel currently possesses only a fraction of the land God promised to Abraham's descendants. The basis for the conflict in the Middle East today is Israel's conviction that all this land belongs to them because of God's covenant with Abraham. But the land will belong to them one day. During Christ's thousand-year reign on the earth, when God fulfills His promise, all the land God promised unconditionally to Abraham will belong to believing Israel.[2]

**God Promised a Nation**

In the second part of God's covenant with Abraham, He promised a nation: "I will make you a great nation, and I will bless you, and make your name great; and so you shall be a blessing" (Genesis 12:2).

Abraham would become the father of a great nation. Even though Abraham was an old man (Hebrews 11:12 describes him as being "as good as dead") and was married to a barren wife (Genesis 11:30), God said he would have not just one descendant, but he would have so many descendants he wouldn't be able to count them all! In Genesis 22:17, God said Abraham's descendants would be as numerous "as the stars of the heavens and as the sand which is on the seashore."

Notice that in this covenant, God also said to Abraham, "I will bless those who bless you, and the one who curses you I will curse" (12:3). We see that throughout history. People who blessed Abraham's descendants, the Jewish people, were blessed by God. Those who cursed Israel and the Jewish people were cursed by God.

In the Old Testament, those who came against Israel—the Egyptians, the Hittites, the Canaanites, the Jebusites—were defeated. The Greeks became a world power, and in 167 BC, under the rule of Antiochus Epiphanes, they desecrated the temple in Jerusalem— and soon after that, they were defeated by the Romans. The Roman Empire was the greatest empire in the world, yet after they destroyed the temple of God in Jerusalem in AD 70, they were reduced to dust. The same thing is true today. Whether it's Poland, Spain, or Great Britain, any nation that is not a friend of God does not stay a great power in the world. I believe one reason God has blessed America in the past is that America has been a friend to Israel.

Why do I support Israel? I not only want to be on the right side of history, but I also want to be on the right side of God. When you support Israel, you are on the right side of God's blessing. We need to support Israel. That doesn't mean everything Israel does is right, but it means when we support Israel's right to inhabit the land God has given them, we can be sure we're on the right side of God.

## God Promised a Blessing

The third part of the Abrahamic covenant is the climax of God's promise. God said to Abraham, "In you all the families of the earth will be blessed" (v. 3). God would not only bless those who blessed Israel, but through Abraham's descendants, He would give a blessing to the entire world.

God was promising that one of Abraham's descendants would be the Savior of the world who would remove the curse of sin and death. This promise is a reference to the Lord Jesus Christ. How do I know this blessing refers to Christ? In the book of Galatians, the apostle Paul said Abraham understood the blessing God gave him in Genesis 12:3 was tied to the coming of Christ: "Even so Abraham believed God, and it was reckoned to him as righteousness. Therefore, be sure that it is those who are of faith who are sons of Abraham. The Scripture, foreseeing that God would justify the Gentiles by faith, preached the gospel beforehand to Abraham, saying, 'All the nations will be blessed in you'" (Galatians 3:6–8).

God promised Abraham that a Savior was coming. And Abraham's faith in that promise was "reckoned . . . to him as righteousness" (Genesis 15:6).

# Three Key Characteristics of the Abrahamic Covenant

Let's look at three characteristics of the Abrahamic covenant that are key to understanding the central role of Israel in the end times.

### God's Promise Is Literal

First of all, I want you to notice that God's promise to Abraham is literal. God promised Abraham an actual piece of real estate that would be his forever. This promised land, Canaan, is not just some metaphor for heaven in the future. It's an actual land that would belong to Abraham.

How do I know that? Look at how Abraham responded to the promise, recorded in Genesis 12:4–5: As soon as he received the promise, "Abram went forth as the LORD had spoken to him; and Lot went with him. Now Abram was seventy-five years old when he departed from Haran. Abram took Sarai his wife and Lot his nephew, and all their possessions which they had accumulated, and the persons which they had acquired in Haran, and they set out for the land of Canaan; thus they came to the land of Canaan." Abraham understood this was a literal promise. He said, "Family, it's time to pack up and move. We're headed to this land." If he thought this promise was talking only about heaven, why would he have gone through all this trouble?

It was a big deal in Abraham's day to move someplace. You couldn't call a moving company and say, "Come pack up our stuff; we're going to Canaan." You had to do it yourself, and notice Abraham had to pack all the things he had accumulated in seventy-five years of living. Do you have a lot of junk around your house? Just recently, we cleaned out our garage. It was amazing the junk we had accumulated in there. Some of it we hauled from our last residence and had hauled from our residence before that; we just carried the junk around with us. At age seventy-five, Abraham surely had a lot of stuff. Why did he go through all that hassle to moving it himself? Because he was headed to a literal land that God has promised him.

Yes, Abraham was looking for heaven too. Hebrews 11:10 says, "For he was looking for the city which has foundations, whose architect and builder is God." But even though Abraham was looking for a heavenly home, that didn't negate the fact that he was looking for an earthly home as well.

## God's Promise Is Eternal

Second, I want you to notice that this promise is eternal. It wasn't just for a specified time. In Genesis 13, God reaffirmed to Abraham that the promised land would belong to him and his descendants forever. Look at Genesis 13:14–15: "The LORD said to Abram, after Lot had separated from him, 'Now lift up your eyes and look from the place where you are, northward and southward and eastward and westward; for all the land which you see, I will give it to you and to your descendants forever.'"

Let me tell you, forever is a long time. We have a hard time as mortal beings understanding what eternity is like. I came across these words from author Hendrik Willem van Loon, who wrote, "High up in the North in the land called Svithjod, there stands a

47

rock. It is a hundred miles high and a hundred miles wide. Once every thousand years a little bird comes to this rock to sharpen its beak. When the rock has thus been worn away, then a single day of eternity will have gone by."[3] Forever is a long time. God said to Abraham, "This land is going to be yours and your believing descendants' forever."

## God's Promise Is Unconditional

Third, and most significantly for Bible prophecy, the Abrahamic covenant is an unconditional promise. Many Christians will concede, "Yes, God promised Abraham a land, descendants, and a blessing, but then Israel, Abraham's descendants, messed up big-time. They rebelled against God and ultimately rejected Christ." These Christians reinterpret the Abrahamic covenant by claiming that God meant to fulfill His promise to Abraham, but when the Jews rejected Jesus Christ, Israel forfeited those blessings. As a result, those blessings have been transferred to the church and transformed into symbolic promises.

What are we to say to that? It's true as you read through Scripture that God made some conditional promises to Israel. Over and over again, God promised Israel blessings for obedience and curses for disobedience. In fact, as Moses prepared the Israelites to enter the promised land, Canaan, God said in Deuteronomy 11:26–28, "See, I am setting before you today a blessing and a curse: the blessing, if you listen to the commandments of the LORD your God, which I am commanding you today; and the curse, if you do not listen to the commandments of the LORD your God, but turn aside from the way which I am commanding you today, by following other gods which you have not known." And all of Israel's history is a story of blessings and curses. When they followed God, they were blessed; when they disobeyed God, they were judged and spent time in calamity and exile. That's all of Israel's history.

But here's one thing to remember: these blessings and curses came through Moses, but the promise came through Abraham. Abraham lived 430 years before Moses. The conditional promises God gave to Moses in no way whatsoever negate the unconditional promises He made to Abraham.

Let me illustrate that for you. After our first daughter was born, Amy and I went to our attorney to make out our will, and we decided at that time that we were going to leave our estate to our children upon our deaths. We didn't know at that time how many children we would have, but we made that decision. That was an unconditional decision. We were going to leave our estate to our children, whoever they were. Now, after our second daughter was born, and both girls started to grow up and mature, we established our own list of blessings and curses around our house. If our girls obeyed what we told them to do, then they were blessed by us; they got their allowance. If they disobeyed us, then they forfeited their allowance and experienced other expressions of wrath from their parents. Growing up in our home, Julia and Dorothy experienced their share of blessings and curses. But it didn't matter whatever they did and whatever temporary consequences they experienced—never once did it cause us to change our will. That was an unconditional promise we had made to them; they were our children and will be our children forever. The promise of their inheritance has nothing to do with their actions; it's nothing that can be changed. It's an irrevocable decision.

In the same way, God's promise to Abraham was an irrevocable decision—it had nothing to do with the Israelites' actions. In Galatians 3:17–18, Paul made this same argument about the unconditional nature of the Abrahamic covenant. He said, "The Law, which came four hundred and thirty years later [through Moses], does not invalidate a covenant previously ratified by God [the Abrahamic covenant], so as to nullify the promise. For if the inheritance is based on law, it is no longer based on a promise; but God has granted it to Abraham by means of a promise." This promise of an inheritance was an irrevocable promise that God made to Abraham and his descendants 430 years before He gave Moses the law. The law came along later. There was a temporary series of blessings and curses. But even though Israel disobeyed God, their actions in no way negated the promise that God had made to Abraham.

Perhaps the greatest evidence of the unconditional nature of the Abrahamic covenant is in the way it was ratified before Abraham in Genesis 15. In Abraham's day, when two kings made a contract with each other, they ratified that contract by taking animals and slicing them down the backbone. They would put one half of each animal on one side and the other half of each animal on the other side, and then the two kings would each take a torch and walk side by side between those animal pieces. It was a way of signifying that this was a bilateral contract, and each king had a responsibility to keep that contract intact. If one of the kings failed to keep his end of the deal, the state of the animals represented what would happen to him: he would lose his life. Each king was saying to the other, "May I lose my life if I don't keep my end of the bargain."

God made a contract with Abraham, but how did Abraham know that God would keep His end of the bargain? God told Abraham to get the animals and slice them (vv. 9–10). Abraham knew the drill. But before Abraham and God walked through the animal pieces together, notice what happened.

Verse 12 says, "Now when the sun was going down, a deep sleep fell upon Abram; and behold, terror and great darkness fell upon him." Then God repeated His covenant to Abraham. And then look at how He ratified this covenant: "It came about when the sun had set, that it was very dark, and behold, there appeared a smoking oven and a flaming torch which passed between these pieces" (v. 17). In other words, after Abraham sliced those animals, God put Abraham to sleep. Abraham was in a deep sleep when God took the torch, and God walked between the animal pieces by Himself.

God was signifying that the fulfillment of this covenant didn't depend on what Abraham did or didn't do; it was an unconditional promise. It depended only on the faithfulness of God. God made this contract not with Abraham but with Himself.

You may be saying, "Pastor, you're reading way too much into that." Look at what the writer of Hebrews said: "For when God made the promise to

Abraham, since He could swear by no one greater, He swore by Himself, saying, 'I will surely bless you and I will surely multiply you'" (6:13–14).

# The Abrahamic Covenant and Israel's Future

What does all this have to do with the end times? Simply this: God promised to Israel a certain land. Since 1948, Israel has been a nation, and they've been in a land, but they haven't been in all of the promised land yet. God has kept the nation of Israel, and they've endured for thousands of years so far, but God is not yet finished with Israel—God is not yet finished with Israel. It's true that God sent a blessing to all the world through Jesus Christ and that He rules in the hearts of individual believers. That's true, but He's not yet sitting on the throne of David in Jerusalem as God promised He would one day (2 Samuel 7:8–16).

God still has some unfinished business here on planet Earth when it comes to the nation of Israel. God is going to keep His literal, eternal, and unconditional promise to Abraham and Abraham's descendants.

# The Abrahamic Covenant and Our Future

You may be saying, "That's wonderful, but I'm not a Jew, so why should I care about the Abrahamic covenant and Israel?" Although the Abrahamic covenant was given to Abraham and his believing descendants, it has ramifications for you and me as well. But, even more importantly, we ought to care whether God keeps His promise to Israel because it's our way of knowing that God is going to keep His promises to us as well.

You see, just as God has made some unconditional promises to the believing Jews, He's made some unconditional promises to you and me that we bank on every day. In John 10:28, Jesus said, "I give eternal life to them, and they will never perish; and no one will snatch them out of My hand." Hebrews 7:25 says, "He is able also to save forever those who draw near to God through Him, since He always lives to make intercession for them." And Hebrews 13:5 records God's promise to us: "I will never desert you, nor will I ever forsake you."

The same God who can be trusted to keep His promises to Israel is the same God we are depending on to keep His unconditional, eternal promise of salvation to us. If God changes His covenant with

Israel, if God revokes the promise He made to Israel, how do we know He won't do the same to us? How do we know that one day, when we stand before Him in judgment, God won't say to us, "Well, I know I told you I was going to save you by grace, but I've changed My mind. Now salvation is based on your works, and you don't have enough." What's to keep God from doing that? It is the character of God Himself. Romans 11:29 says, "For the gifts and the calling of God are irrevocable." And just as we can depend upon the character of God to secure the unconditional promise He has made to us, we can trust that God is going to keep His unconditional promise to Abraham and his descendants—a promise that has ramifications for the world in the years ahead.

When I stood outside the US embassy in Jerusalem on its opening day, I ended my prayer by echoing the prayer of the psalmist: "Pray for the peace of Jerusalem! . . . 'Peace be within your walls and security within your towers!" (Psalm 122:6–7 ESV). In these last days, we should support Israel fully while praying fervently that peace will come soon. Though many will assail Israel and the Jewish people, we know that these satanic schemes will always be fruitless. God has promised that Israel will endure forever. God is faithful. He always tells the truth. Every promise He has made to Israel will be fulfilled![4]

# 3

# What News Events Signal the End Times?

In my lifetime, I have never sensed so much unrest in the world. It seems that every day brings a new set of terrifying headlines. Everywhere I go, people are sensing that something big is about to happen. Will there be another 9/11-style attack on America? Will radical Islamic terrorists succeed in creating a Muslim caliphate in the Middle East? Will some other supervirus spread across America and the world? Will Christians be jailed for their faith not just in other countries but here as well? Will we ever trust our own government again? Is the world itself unraveling before our eyes?

We have no idea when the end is going to happen. God hasn't given us a date, but He does want us to be aware of the events that will lead up to Jesus's return so that we can be sober, on the alert, and ready for his appearing.

# Three Extremes to Avoid in Bible Prophecy

Whenever we look at current events in light of biblical prophecy, there are at least three extremes we need to avoid.

## Fanaticism

First of all, we need to avoid the extreme I call fanaticism. You know, since the beginning of the world, people have tried to predict the end of the world. In chapter 1, I gave you a list of end-times predictions that all proved false, showing how foolish it is to engage in date setting. So the idea that current events appear to be lining up with the end times is nothing new.

As we have seen, Jesus said in Matthew 24:36, "But of that day and hour no one knows, not even the angels of heaven, nor the Son, but the Father alone." We can't know the time, but God wants us to be aware of the times. We need to avoid fanaticism.

## Fatalism

A second extreme to avoid—and one that appears to be more prevalent in the church today—is fatalism. It's the attitude that says, "Well, the world's going to hell in a handbasket, and Christ is coming back.

There's nothing I can do to change that, so why bother about anything happening in the world? Why stand up and push back against evil if all these terrible things are going to lead to the return of Jesus Christ anyway? Why not just sit back and wait for the end to happen?" That's what I see happening with many Christians today.

Let me remind you of something: just because an event is inevitable does not mean it's immediate. For example, I know it's inevitable that one day I'm going to die, and there's nothing I'm going to do to change that. Unless the rapture happens first, we're all going to die someday. But the fact that death is inevitable doesn't keep me from exercising, going to the doctor, and eating bran flakes every morning for breakfast. Why do I do that? It's not because I'm afraid of dying. I know death is inevitable, but I want to prolong my life so that I can fulfill God's purpose for me here on earth.

It's the same way with the world situation. There's a reason we ought to stand up and push back against evil. There's a reason we ought to stand for God's truth. We ought to take action so that we can prevent the premature implosion of this world and have longer to share the gospel of Jesus Christ with as many people as possible. The fact that Christ is coming back again should not motivate us to inaction; it ought to motivate us to action. Knowing that the end is coming ought to make us work that much harder. Jesus said, "We must work the works of Him who sent Me as long as it is day; night is coming when no one can work" (John 9:4). As Christians, we ought to be the ones on the forefront of the action in this world.

## Cynicism

The third extreme we need to avoid when considering current events in light of the end times is the most dangerous of all, and that's cynicism. Some people have been hardened to the idea of Christ coming back again. They say, "People have been saying for two thousand years that Jesus is coming back again. It hasn't happened yet. Don't be fooled." But the apostle Peter reminded us, "With the Lord one day is like a thousand years, and a thousand years like one day" (2 Peter 3:8). The fact is, Jesus's return to earth was a major subject of His teaching.

Jesus is coming back again, and He's coming back for everyone to see. In Matthew 24:27, He said, "Just as the lightning comes from the east and flashes even to the west, so will the coming of the Son of Man be."

It's important for us to look at the events that are happening in the world today through the lens of Bible prophecy. Remember, although we can't know the time, God wants us to understand the times in which we live so that we as the people of God can be prepared for His return. In 1 Thessalonians 5:6, Paul said, "Let us not sleep as others do, but let us be alert and sober"—in other words, alert to what is happening in the world today. Karl Barth once told some young theologians, "Take your Bible and take your newspaper"—today it might be your Facebook newsfeed—"and read both. But interpret newspapers from your Bible." The newspaper tells you what is happening in the world, but the Bible tells you what it means.[1]

# Five Signs of the End Times

In Matthew 24, Jesus and His disciples were on the Mount of Olives after visiting the temple in Jerusalem. On their way out of the temple, Jesus had said, "Truly I say to you, not one stone here [the temple] will be left upon another, which will not be torn down" (v. 2). So when they got to the Mount of Olives, the disciples asked Him privately, "Tell us, when will these things happen, and what will be the sign of Your coming, and of the end of the age?" (v. 3).

How did Jesus respond to their question? He could have told them, "Mind your own business." He could have said, "This isn't important for you to know about. You leave the end times up to Me, and just concentrate on your walk with God." Instead, Jesus answered their question not with a date but with a detailed explanation of the events that would lead to His return. In this passage, Jesus gave five signs that will precede His return.

As we look briefly at each of these five signs, remember that while in one sense we're seeing many of these things take place right now, it's also true that throughout history many of these things have taken place. Jesus was saying that before He comes, these things are going to increase in intensity and frequency. What are the five signs?

## Spiritual Deception

The first sign Jesus mentioned is spiritual deception. In Matthew 24:4–5, He said to His disciples, "See to it that no one misleads you. For many will come in My name, saying, 'I am the Christ,' and will mislead many." Now, in every age there have been religious charlatans and hucksters. Implied in Jesus's words is this reality: as we get closer to the end, we're going to see the number of these false teachers increase. In fact, toward the end, many will actually claim to be Christ Himself.

Look carefully at what the apostle Paul wrote

to Timothy in 1 Timothy 4:1. He said, "The Spirit explicitly says that in later times some will fall away from the faith, paying attention to deceitful spirits and doctrines of demons." As we get closer to the end times, we'll see a rise in satanism and the occult. And we're seeing that right now.[2]

All this deception by Satan and his demons will come to a climax during the tribulation when the Antichrist, the great world leader, will be empowered by Satan to perform signs and wonders in order to deceive some people. In 2 Thessalonians 2:9, Paul explained that the Antichrist will come "in accord with the activity of Satan, with all power and signs and false wonders." Make no mistake about it: Satan has the ability to perform miracles. Just because a miracle occurs doesn't mean it necessarily comes from God. For whatever reason, God has given Satan limited authority to perform signs and wonders in order to deceive those people who have hardened their hearts against God. In the end times, we will see this spiritual deception on the increase, culminating with the Antichrist.

## International Conflict

The second sign that Jesus described is international conflict. In Matthew 24:6–7, He said, "You will be hearing of wars and rumors of wars. See that you are not frightened, for those things must take place, but that is not yet the end. For nation will rise against nation, and kingdom against kingdom." Leon Trotsky reportedly said, "Whoever among us longs for a quiet life has certainly chosen the wrong epoch."[3] Do you know when Trotsky, a Marxist philosopher and the founder of the Red Army, made this statement? About a hundred years ago. The world wasn't peaceful in his day, and it's not peaceful today either.

See if any of these names look familiar to you: Iraq, Syria, Ukraine, Hong Kong, the East China Sea, Crimea, Chechnya, Serbia, Kosovo, Lebanon, Iraq, Kashmir, Somalia, Yemen, Israel, Gaza, and the West Bank. These are just a few of the hot spots in the world. Eighty years ago, American troops were fighting in Germany and Japan. Then they moved to Korea. Then Vietnam. And now they've moved to the Persian Gulf and other areas in the Middle East. We can add Afghanistan and Pakistan to the list of countries, and who knows how many other Middle Eastern countries will be added to the list in the coming years. We're seeing international conflict on an unprecedented scale, and Jesus said this is a sign of His soon return.

### Natural Disasters

Third, Jesus said that natural disasters will precede His coming. In Matthew 24:7, He said, "In various places there will be famines and earthquakes." Think about what we have seen in the world lately—widespread famines caused by weather and war, as well as horrifying earthquakes that have killed thousands of people. In verse 8, Jesus went on to say, "But all these things are merely the beginning of birth pangs."

Interestingly, in a similar discourse recorded in Luke 21:11, Jesus added the word "pestilences" (KJV) to the list of natural disasters. I hate to admit it, but for years I read that and thought, *Well, He must mean something like locusts or boll weevils.* But the word translated "pestilences" in the King James Version, or "plagues" in the New American Standard Version, refers to an outbreak of a disease on an epidemic level. That's what Jesus was talking about—the outbreak of disease. Think about what we've experienced in our lifetimes so far with smallpox, botulism, Ebola, and COVID-19—and who knows what will happen in the future. Jesus said pandemics like these are going to be one of the signs that precede His return.

### Persecution of Christians

Number four, Jesus said His return will be marked by fierce persecution of believers. In Matthew 24:9,

He said, "Then they will deliver you to tribulation, and will kill you, and you will be hated by all nations because of My name." You know, I don't know a single Christian who has memorized that verse and claimed it as his life verse. Most people don't want to focus on that. It's not a very pleasant thought. But if you believe the words of Jesus, you have to take this seriously. Jesus said before He returns, there is going to be mass persecution of believers.

We're seeing that happen on the world stage right now. How can anybody deny that Islam is a violent religion? Terrorists kill in the name of Islam. They butcher people in the name of Islam. They burn churches down in the name of Islam. They do it all as a way to worship their false god, Allah. This is what a large segment of modern Islam has become—a violent religion that hates Christians and Jews. (More about radical Islam related to Bible prophecy in appendix A, "The Rise of Radical Islam.")

I'm not saying the majority of Muslims are terrorists, but when even 5 percent of Muslims embrace, that means there are at least eighty-five million radical Muslims in the world who want to persecute the people of God.[4]

It is time for us to speak up and say, "Enough is enough." It's time for us to quit being silent about the mass persecution of our brothers and sisters in Christ around the world. All of this is a sign of the soon return of Christ. And by the way, the persecution we're seeing happen around the world is getting ready to land on the shores of America as well. The seeds are being sown right now. Get ready for it, and stay grounded in the truth of God's Word so you will be able to stand firm when your faith is tested.

## Widespread Apostasy

Fifth, Jesus said another sign of His return will be widespread apostasy. Look at Matthew 24:10–12: "At that time many will fall away and will betray one another and hate one another. Many false prophets will arise and will mislead many. Because lawlessness is increased, most people's love will grow cold." In this passage, the term translated "fall away" refers to apostasy. Jesus was saying, "One of the signs of My return is that people will fall away from their faith."

Now, think about this: the only people who can fall away from faith are people who once believed something or professed to believe something. Atheists don't fall away from faith to unfaith; they are already in unfaith. They can't fall any further. When Jesus talked about apostasy, He was talking about people who claim to be believers, people who claim to believe the Bible, but in the last days they will fall away from that faith and try to lead astray as many people as possible.

We are seeing that happen today in evangelical churches across this country. We see churches that in the name of unity say, "We no longer believe the Bible is the inspired and inerrant Word of God. We no longer claim that Jesus was born of a virgin. We no longer believe in the blood atonement of Christ for the sins of the world. We no longer believe that Jesus is the only way to salvation. We have a more inclusive message." These churches are leading people astray.

Today, we also see Christian churches that in the name of love are starting to say, "We no longer are going to stand up against certain things. We're not going to stand up against a woman's right to choose abortion. We're not going to stand up against same-sex marriage. We're only going to stand for love." That's the kind of apostasy that Jesus said would mark His return.

## Our Response to News Events

How have you been responding to disturbing news events during these last days? Are you allowing the cable news pundits to paralyze you with fear? Are you depending on some politician or political movement to reverse the downward spiral of this country? Or are you simply trying to ignore the chaos and take care of yourself and your family until the end comes?

God has called each of us to a much greater purpose than simply trying to eke out a living and bide our time until Jesus returns. God has called all Christians to stand up and push back against evil in our culture during these last days. In the time that remains before we meet Jesus, we're not to be fearful or apathetic. Instead, we are to be the force that is willing to stand up and illuminate this ever-darkening world with the light of the gospel of Jesus Christ. As we see the signs of the end times continue to increase in intensity and frequency in the coming days, the opportunity and need for us to share God's truth has never been greater.[5]

# 4

# What Are the Major Events of the End Times?

*S poiler alert: this chapter gives away the ending—
not just of the Bible but of the earth, the heavens,
and all created beings. If you don't want to know
what happens, stop reading now.*

A disclaimer like this likely wouldn't deter many
people from reading further, because most of us want
to know how things are going to turn out—even if we
may be peeking through our fingers at some of it.

## An Extraordinary Glimpse of the Future

As a planner by nature, I like to set clear goals for my
personal life, family life, and ministry. There are certain
things I intend to accomplish in the short term and
in the long term. I like to know what's ahead of me.
But the reality is, no matter how many plans I make,
I don't actually know what will happen tomorrow,

much less ten years from now.

As finite creatures, you and I are hopelessly limited by our vantage point in time. We can look backward at the past, but we can't see any further forward than this moment. To have any grasp of future events, we must rely on the one who is eternal.

Throughout the Bible—especially in the book of Revelation—God helps us see what we cannot see on our own. He gives us an apocalyptic yet hope-filled vision of how the final days of His original creation will play out. In this chapter, I will give you an easy-to-understand preview of God's plan for these last days and the coming end times.

# Understanding the Timeline

With thousands of end-times prophecies to consider, the task of sorting and understanding them may seem monumental. But that task is made much easier by the fact that the Bible's prophecies align in a way that reveals a specific timeline of future events.[1] This timeline, which begins with the present age and extends to eternity, gives us an excellent starting point in understanding the future God has planned.

Let's take a look at some of the key events on the timeline.

## The Church Age

If the church age seems familiar to you, it's because you're living in it, some two thousand years after it began. The church age is the period of time from Pentecost until the rapture (which we will discuss further in the next section), during which Gentiles are invited to participate in the blessings of the covenant God made with Abraham and his descendants in Genesis 12. In the church age, God has extended the "invitation list" to be part of God's kingdom beyond the Jews to include anyone who will accept His offer of salvation.

Throughout the Old Testament, God continually worked to draw His people into a right relationship with Him. But they resisted Him time and time again. Finally, in the New Testament, God sent His own Son, the long-promised Messiah, to accomplish the work of salvation. How did Israel respond to Jesus Christ? Most of God's people rejected Him.

But God would not allow them to thwart His plan. He wanted people to acknowledge and worship His Son, so He temporarily turned away from His people, the Israelites, and invited Gentiles to share in His blessing. That invitation ushered in the church age.

So here's where we stand right now: God has

temporarily set aside the people of Israel because they rejected His Son. He has given the rest of the world an opportunity to be included in His covenant with Abraham. However, Paul made clear in Romans 11:1 that God is not through with Israel yet: "I say then, God has not rejected His people, has He? May it never be!" In verse 7, Paul referred to Israel's attitude as being "hardened." But it's a temporary hardening— one that will last until every Gentile whom God has ordained to be saved is saved. After that, Israel will be given one final chance. Until that time, we're living in the church age. And it will continue until the rapture of the church.

## The Rapture of the Church

The Greek word from which we get our word *rapture* means "to snatch away." And for those who are left behind after the rapture of the church, that's probably what the event will seem like. In a single moment, all Christians, from the time of Pentecost until the moment the rapture occurs, will be caught up to meet the Lord in the air. In 1 Thessalonians 4:16–17, Paul described it this way: "For the Lord Himself will descend from heaven with a shout, with the voice of the archangel and with the trumpet of God, and the dead in Christ will rise first. Then we who are alive and remain will be caught up together with them in the clouds to meet the Lord in the air, and so we shall always be with the Lord."

There are four details in Paul's description that bear examination. The first is that, while Jesus will descend from heaven, He will not come all the way to the earth. He will descend into the sky, and that's where we will meet Him. The rapture will be a midair gathering.

The second detail is that all Christians who have died since the day of Pentecost will be raised. When Christians die, our bodies remain on earth, but our spirits go to be with the Lord. That's what Paul was talking about when he wrote, "To be absent from the body [is] to be at home with the Lord" (2 Corinthians 5:8). But our separation from our bodies is only temporary. When the rapture occurs, graves will be opened and the bodies of the saved will be raised.

The third detail is that Christians who are alive when the rapture occurs will meet the Lord in the air as living beings. That means an entire generation of believers will never experience death. They will pass directly from life in this world to life in the next.

The fourth detail is that our bodies will be changed from mortal to immortal. Paul said, "This mortal must put on immortality" (1 Corinthians 15:53). At the rapture, believers will receive brand-new resurrection bodies from God that are free from pain, suffering, and sickness.

Perhaps the most pertinent aspect of the rapture is its imminence. There are no prophecies that must take place before it can occur. In short, the rapture can happen at any moment.

## The Judgment Seat of Christ

Contrary to what some people believe, there is not one final judgment that includes both believers and unbelievers. Unbelievers will be judged at the great white throne judgment (Revelation 20:11–15), which we will look at in a moment. But Christians will be judged at the judgment seat of Christ, which probably occurs immediately after the rapture.

Paul described this coming evaluation of believers' lives: "We also have as our ambition, whether at home or absent, to be pleasing to Him. For we must all appear before the judgment seat of Christ, so that each one may be recompensed for his deeds in the body, according to what he has done, whether good or bad" (2 Corinthians 5:9–10).

Believers will one day answer to Christ for every thought, word, action, and motivation of our earthly lives. But unlike the great white throne judgment for unbelievers, the purpose of the judgment seat of Christ is not condemnation but evaluation and commendation. At the judgment seat of Christ, our lives will be evaluated by Christ—not to determine our eternal destination, since that was sealed at the moment of our salvation, but to determine our rewards in heaven.

## The Tribulation

The tribulation is a seven-year period that will begin when a world leader, who is referred to in Scripture as the beast or Antichrist, signs a peace treaty with Israel. The tribulation will end with the second coming of Christ.

The seven-year timeframe of the tribulation is significant in biblical prophecy. It can be traced back to a promise God made in Daniel 9. When the Israelites were in exile in Babylon, the angel Gabriel revealed to Daniel that there were 490 years left on God's stopwatch to finish His plan with Israel and usher in the millennium. The angel referred to the timeframe as seventy weeks, with each year represented as a day. Seventy weeks times seven years equals 490 years.

However, there would be a separation between the first 483 years and the final seven years—that is, between the first sixty-nine weeks and the seventieth week. Gabriel explained that God would start the countdown when a decree was issued for the Israelites to rebuild Jerusalem. We know from history that this decree was issued on March 14, 445 BC.

According to Gabriel, the time from that decree until the Messiah was presented would be 483 years. On April 2, AD 32—exactly 483 years after the decree to rebuild Jerusalem—Jesus rode on a donkey through the streets of Jerusalem, and people recognized Him as the Messiah.

Gabriel further explained that the Messiah would be cut off—or crucified. After that, there would be a gap of time before the final seven years commenced. That's where we are right now. On God's stopwatch, 483 years have passed. There are seven years left for God to complete His plan for Israel, which He will do during the tribulation. His stopwatch will begin again after the rapture, as soon as the Antichrist signs a peace treaty with Israel.

The tribulation will fulfill two purposes. The first is the salvation of Israel. At the beginning of the seven-year period, God will save 144,000 Jews, who will serve as His witnesses throughout the tribulation. Through the work and testimony of those witnesses, many Jews—and even some Gentiles—will be saved.

The second purpose of the tribulation is the condemnation of unbelievers living on earth. The seven-year period will be a time of unprecedented judgment against the world by God. In Revelation 6–19, John identified three series of judgments God will pour out on the earth—seal judgments, trumpet judgments, and bowl judgments—each more devastating than the last.

## Armageddon and the Second Coming of Christ

According to Revelation 19, at the end of the tribulation, all the world's military forces will gather on the plain of Megiddo in Israel to wage war against the Antichrist and his forces. This final world conflict is called the battle of Armageddon.

But as the armies prepare to destroy one another, suddenly their attention will be diverted upward to a sight they will never recover from—the second coming of Christ. Here's how the apostle John described it in Revelation 19:11, 14–16: "I saw heaven opened, and behold, a white horse, and He who sat on it is called Faithful and True, and in righteousness He judges and wages war. . . . And the armies which are in heaven, clothed in fine linen, white and clean, were following Him on white horses. From His mouth comes a sharp sword, so that with it He may strike down the nations, and He will rule them with a rod of iron; and He treads the wine press of the fierce wrath of God, the

Almighty. And on His robe and on His thigh He has a name written, 'King of kings, and Lord of lords.'" When Christ returns, the tribulation will come to an end. All unbelievers alive at that time will be cast into eternal punishment (Matthew 25:46), but believers who put their faith in Christ during the tribulation and survive to see His return will be ushered into the millennium.

## The Millennium

The millennium is a thousand-year period that will occur after the second coming. For one thousand years, Jesus Christ will reign on earth, fulfilling God's promise to Abraham in Genesis 15. God promised Abraham that his believing descendants would one day possess a land where the Messiah would rule on the throne of David from Jerusalem. Abraham believed Him, and so did his descendants. For centuries, the people of Israel clung to the hope of that promise.

As the days of creation wind to a close, God will demonstrate His faithfulness again. And it's vital that we understand the significance of this fulfillment. After all, if God were to renege on—or even slightly alter—His promise to Israel, what would keep Him from doing the same thing with the promise He made to us of eternal life?

Christ will initiate His thousand-year reign by asserting His power over His foes, as described in Revelation 20:1–3: "Then I saw an angel coming down from heaven. . . . And he laid hold of the dragon, the serpent of old, who is the devil and Satan, and bound him for a thousand years; and he threw him into the abyss, and shut it and sealed it over him, so that he would not deceive the nations any longer, until the thousand years were completed."

With Satan bound for a thousand years, part of the curse of sin will be removed. This is the time Isaiah 65 describes, when infants will not die, when people will live to be at least one hundred years old, and when we won't have difficulty in agriculture with thorns and thistles. The millennium will see a renovation, but not a re-creation, of the earth.

## Satan Released and the Final Rebellion

At the end of the millennium, Satan will be released "for a short time" (Revelation 20:3). The question is, Why would God let him go, especially when things will be going so well?

Here's what we need to understand: only believers will enter the millennium and experience the earthly reign of Christ. Those of us who were saved before the tribulation, along with the people who became believers during the tribulation and then died, will enter the millennium in our new, resurrected bodies. But people who became believers during the tribulation and survived until Christ's second coming will enter the millennium in their natural bodies. That means they will be able to marry and have children. During the thousand-year reign of Christ on earth, children will be born, grow up, and have families of their own, for generation after generation.

Keep in mind, too, that it's necessary that every person choose whether to follow Jesus. So at the end of the thousand years, God will release Satan for a short time and allow him to work his evil influence. Amazingly, some people who were born and grew up during the millennium will choose to follow Satan instead of Jesus. That is the final rebellion.

## The Great White Throne Judgment

God will put an end to this rebellion once and for all at the great white throne judgment—His final judgment against all unbelievers who have ever lived. In Revelation 20:13, John described the scene this way: "And the sea gave up the dead which were in it, and death and Hades gave up the dead which were in them; and they were judged, every one of them according to their deeds." When unbelievers die, their spirits go to hades, which is described as a place of agony (Luke 16:24). Hades is a temporary place of intense suffering for the unsaved dead as they await their final judgment.

At the great white throne judgment, all the unbelieving dead will appear before the Lord and be judged by their works. That criterion is only fair, since unbelievers say, in effect, "I don't need God's forgiveness; I'm good enough to get into heaven on my own merit." So God agrees to their terms and judges them by their works. Unfortunately, the standard by which God judges is the perfection of Jesus Christ. And by that standard, "all . . . fall short of the glory of God" (Romans 3:23).

The result of this judgment is spelled out in Revelation 20:14–15, when "death and Hades were thrown into the lake of fire. This is the second death, the lake of fire. And if anyone's name was not found written in the book of life, he was thrown into the lake of fire." Verse 10 completes the picture: "They will be tormented day and night forever and ever."

Unbelievers will not be destroyed after they are judged; instead, they will suffer for eternity. The same Greek word that is used to describe the eternal nature of heaven is also used to describe the eternal nature of hell. The horrible truth about hell is this: when you've spent three trillion years in the agony of hell, you will not have reduced by one second the amount of time you have left. That's the fate of everyone who dies without trusting in Jesus Christ.

According to 2 Peter 3:7, 10, one final event will conclude the great white throne judgment: "By His word the present heavens and earth are being reserved for fire, kept for the day of judgment and destruction of ungodly men. . . . But the day of the Lord will come like a thief, in which the heavens will pass away with a roar and the elements will be destroyed with intense heat, and the earth and its works will be burned up."

## Eternity Future

After the present heaven and earth are destroyed, we come to the events in Revelation 21. Eternity future begins. Describing his astonishing vision, the apostle John said, "Then I saw a new heaven and a new earth; for the first heaven and the first earth passed away, and there is no longer any sea. And I saw the holy city, new Jerusalem, coming down out of heaven from God, made ready as a bride adorned for her husband" (vv. 1–2).

Popular images of heaven feature believers worshiping God in an ethereal, cloudlike setting. However, as John's vision in Revelation 21 makes clear, the reality of heaven will be much more familiar to us. Our eternal dwelling place will be a new earth. Though in many ways it will seem familiar to us, it will also be very different from the earth we know. It won't be the renovated earth of the millennium. The earth on which we will spend eternity will be entirely re-created, restored to its original purpose. God will allow us to enjoy forever the world as He originally created it to be.[2]

Amazingly, our enjoyment of eternity will be enhanced by the work we do. Humans were created to find fulfillment and joy in work. Contrary to what many people believe, work is not a curse from God as a result of Adam and Eve's sin in the garden. Before the first couple ever took a bite of the forbidden fruit, God gave them the responsibility of work. Genesis 2:15 describes it like this: "Then the LORD God took the man and put him into the garden of Eden to cultivate it and keep it."

Although Eden was perfect, it was not self-sustaining. Humans were given the responsibility of cultivating it by tilling the soil and planting and harvesting crops. While it's true that Adam and Eve's work became much harder after the fall because of God's judgment, work has always been—and will always be—part of God's plan for us.

The only reason we recoil from the prospect of working for eternity is that our labor on earth has been burdened by the effects of sin's curse: bodies that grow tired, relationships that become strained, and an environment that is uncooperative. In the new heaven and earth, all those burdens will disappear because "there will no longer be any curse" (Revelation 22:3). In the world as we know it, work can be exhausting. In eternity, work will be exhilarating.

In eternity, our physical, mental, emotional, and spiritual well-being will be assured. Our resurrected bodies will be perfect. Cancer, heart attacks, and strokes will all be things of the past. So will blindness, deafness, and paralysis, as well as gray hair, wrinkles, and widening girths. From the top of our heads to the bottom of our feet, we'll be perfect in every way.

In eternity, God will "wipe away every tear from [our] eyes; and there will no longer be any death; there will no longer be any mourning, or crying, or pain; the first things have passed away" (21:4). This is the forever future God has planned for those who trust in Jesus Christ.[3]

# 5

# What Is the Difference between the Rapture and the Second Coming in the End Times?

The Bible says we, as Christians, don't have to fear the end times because it will be preceded by an event called the rapture of the church. This event will mark the end of our current church age and usher in the end times, beginning with seven-year period known as the tribulation.

Some people are understandably confused about the two returns of Christ on the prophecy timeline. There are similarities between the rapture and the second coming. However, the differences between the two events are quite pronounced. Let's look at what the Bible says about the rapture and what the Bible says about the second coming, and then we'll observe some of the differences between these two events.

# The Rapture

In 1 Thessalonians 4:16–17, Paul described the rapture of the church: "For the Lord Himself will descend from heaven with a shout, with the voice of the archangel and with the trumpet of God, and the dead in Christ will rise first. Then we who are alive and remain will be caught up together with them in the clouds to meet the Lord in the air, and so we shall always be with the Lord." That phrase "caught up," *harpazo* in Greek, is translated into English as *rapture*. This is the rapture of the church, when Jesus snatches up all Christians to be in heaven with Him before the tribulation.

## When Will the Rapture Occur?

Not all Christians agree on the timing of the rapture.

Some Christians hold to a *midtribulation rapture* view. They believe Christians will be present during the first three and a half years of the tribulation, but they will be caught up to meet the Lord in the air before the most intense suffering occurs.

Some Christians hold to a *posttribulation rapture* view. They believe the snatching away of believers will occur at the end of the seven-year tribulation and will be almost concurrent with the second coming of Christ.

Many other Christians, like myself, hold to a *pretribulation rapture* view. We believe the rapture will occur before the tribulation, that Christians will be spared the torment of those seven years because we are safe and secure from God's wrath.

## Three Reasons for a Pretribulation Rapture

There are at least three reasons to believe that the rapture will take place before the tribulation begins.

*The Promise of God.* The first reason is Jesus's promise that the church will be kept from the tribulation. As Noah was saved from the flood and Lot was saved from the judgment on Sodom and Gomorrah, so believers in Christ will be saved from the wrath that is to come (2 Peter 2:5–9).

Paul told the Thessalonian church to "wait for [God's] Son from heaven, whom He raised from the dead, that is Jesus, who rescues us from the wrath to come. . . . For God has not destined us for wrath, but for obtaining salvation through our Lord Jesus Christ" (1 Thessalonians 1:10; 5:9).

And if this isn't enough of a promise, Jesus said in Revelation 3:10, "Because you have kept the word of My perseverance, I also will keep you from the hour of testing, that hour which is about to come upon the whole world, to test those who dwell on the earth."

This was a promise to the church of Philadelphia, but it's clear that Jesus was also making this promise to the entire church before a coming time of worldwide testing. Jesus was saying there is a group of Christians who will be kept *from* (the Greek word *ek* means "out of") the worldwide testing that is yet to come. The promise of God is that we do not have to fear His wrath. That doesn't mean Christians are exempt from suffering or experiencing persecution, but we never have to fear the wrath of God.

*The Absence of the Church in Revelation 6–18.* The church is prominent in the early chapters of Revelation, either on earth (Revelation 1–3) or in heaven (Revelation 4–5), but it is entirely absent in the chapters covering God's fierce judgments during the tribulation (Revelation 6–18). In fact, after Revelation 5, the church isn't mentioned again until Revelation 19:7, and then we are referred to as "His bride." Why is it that through all of those detailed descriptions of what is happening on earth in Revelation 6–18 there is not one mention of the church? It's because the church isn't on earth. This isn't to say that there are no saved individuals on earth during the tribulation. There are. Many people will come to faith in Christ after the rapture, but they are not considered part of the church.

*The Purpose of the Tribulation.* There is a twofold purpose of the tribulation. The first purpose is the salvation of Israel. Daniel 9 reveals that God will give Israel one last chance to respond. It's an act of God's mercy to motivate them to repentance. The second purpose is the condemnation of unbelievers. God will pour out His wrath on unbelievers, and the tribulation is the time that happens on earth before an eternity in hell. Neither purpose is meant for the church.

Every person who is part of the church has already been saved and does not need to fear the wrath of God. If we have to fear some future punishment of God, then the death of Jesus Christ was absolutely worthless. But it wasn't worthless. Jesus absorbed in some inexplicable way the punishment that you and I deserve. That's why Romans 8:1 promises, "Therefore there is now no condemnation for those who are in Christ Jesus."

I remember hearing the story about a group of cowboys who were out on the prairie, and suddenly they saw a giant fire raging toward them. Not having any way of escape, they resigned themselves to the fact that they were doomed. But one of the cowboys had an idea. He said, "Quick, let's light a fire and burn the ground around us." The other men thought he had lost his mind until he added this word of explanation: "The fire cannot come where it has already been."

Friend, the fire of judgment has already come on Jesus Christ. We don't ever have to worry about it coming again. The promise of God is we don't have to fear the wrath of God that is about to come upon the whole earth, and that is why I am convinced that Christians are going to be raptured before the end-times tribulation.

# The Second Coming

The fact is certain: Jesus Christ is returning to earth one day to reward the righteous and to punish the unrighteous. And it is the only hope that we have.

### Why Is the Second Coming of Christ Necessary?

I want to give you four reasons a literal second coming of Christ is so important.[1]

First, Christ's second coming is necessary *to fulfill promises made in the Bible.* If Christ doesn't return, many prophecies will not be fulfilled, rendering God's Word untrustworthy. Did you know there are eighteen hundred references in the Old Testament to the second coming? In fact, for every prophecy about Christ's first coming, there are eight about His second coming. In the New Testament, there are more than three hundred references to the return of Jesus Christ. The second coming is not just incidental; it's essential.

It is the theme of the entire Bible.

Second, the second coming of Christ is necessary *to judge unbelievers for sin.* If Christ doesn't return, then sin and wickedness will increase and intensify.

Third, Christ's second coming is necessary *to depose Satan from his earthly dominion.* If Christ doesn't return, then Satan will continue to lord over the earth, bringing greater destruction and death. If Christ doesn't come back to reclaim this earth, then Satan has won. Do you think God is going to allow Satan to do that? Not on your life!

Finally, Christ must come again *to establish His kingdom on earth.* If Christ doesn't return, then the earth will never know justice, righteousness, and peace. Over and over again, the Bible promises that the Son of God will return to rule this earth in justice and righteousness in His thousand-year millennial kingdom. Don't you look forward to that day when this earth will finally be what God intended it to be?

This is why Jesus Christ must return, which is described in Revelation 19.

## The Triumphal Entry of the King

Revelation 19:1–10 sets the stage for the return of Jesus Christ, when Jesus comes back to earth with His bride to establish His millennial kingdom. But before they get to earth, all the enemies of the Groom and the bride have to be extinguished.

That's what we see happening in the second half of Revelation 19: the seven-year tribulation is drawing to an end. The Antichrist rose to power during the first half of the tribulation, and the unbelievers on earth were grateful for his leadership. But after three and a half years, the Antichrist began to persecute Israel and the believers who were on the earth. During that time, God's judgments against the earth intensified, and those over whom the Antichrist was reigning got sick and tired of all the bad things that were happening. Revelation 16:12–16 says the kings of the earth gathered to overthrow the Antichrist in the valley of Armageddon.

## A Description of the Coming King

The world's forces are fighting to overthrow the Antichrist when they look up into the sky and see the warrior King, Jesus Christ. Suddenly, that divided human army unites to fight against Christ. That's where we read about the coming King:

> And I saw heaven opened, and behold, a white horse, and He who sat on it is called Faithful and True, and in righteousness He

judges and wages war. His eyes are a flame
of fire, and on His head are many diadems;
and He has a name written on Him which
no one knows except Himself. He is clothed
with a robe dipped in blood, and His name
is called The Word of God. And the armies
which are in heaven, clothed in fine linen,
white and clean, were following Him on
white horses. From His mouth comes a sharp
sword, so that with it He may strike down
the nations, and He will rule them with a
rod of iron; and He treads the wine press
of the fierce wrath of God, the Almighty.
And on His robe and on His thigh He has a
name written, "King of kings, and Lord of
lords." (Revelation 19:11–16)

The King's eyes are blazing fire, symbolizing His
piercing judgment. The "many diadems" are regal
crowns symbolizing His right to rule. It was this
picture that caused Matthew Bridges to write the great
hymn with the opening line, "Crown Him with many
crowns, the Lamb upon His throne."[1]

The King also has a name that only He knows.
The blood on His robe is not His own but the blood
of His enemies on earth who are fighting Him. His

coming was anticipated in Zechariah 14:3–4, which describes Jesus returning to earth at the Mount of Olives, causing such a reaction that the mount will split in two. This is the second coming of the Lord Jesus Christ.

## A Description of the King's Army

In Revelation 19:14, John described the King's army that accompanies Him: "And the armies which are in heaven, clothed in fine linen, white and clean, were following Him on white horses." This army from heaven that follows Him is the church. It is you and me. How do I know that? A few verses earlier, the church is described as clothed "in fine linen," which is "the righteous acts of the saints" (v. 8). The army is the church, and the church is the bride of Christ, who is making herself ready for the wedding.

## A Description of the Warrior King

The final description in Revelation 19:15–16 is that of Jesus the warrior King: "From His mouth comes a sharp sword, so that with it He may strike down the nations, and He will rule them with a rod of iron; and He treads the wine press of the fierce wrath of God, the Almighty. And on His robe and on His thigh He has a name written, 'King of kings, and Lord of lords.'"

That "sharp sword" is the Word of God, which is "living and active and sharper than any two-edged sword" (Hebrews 4:12). The Word of God brings life to those who believe it, and it brings eternal death to those who reject it.

John then picked up the image of pressing grapes used in Revelation 14 to describe God's fierce wrath on sin: "He treads the wine press of the fierce wrath of God, the Almighty" (Revelation 19:15). At God's appointed time, Jesus Christ will trample the grapes of wrath. He is going to bring judgment to all the unbelievers on earth, and their blood will splatter forth like the juice from an overly ripe grape. In fact, at the battle of Armageddon, the death will be so great that blood will splatter up to the bridle of a horse (14:20). This is a fulfilment of Jude 14–15: "Behold, the Lord came with many thousands of His holy ones, to execute judgment upon all, and to convict all the ungodly of all their ungodly deeds which they have done in an ungodly way, and of all the harsh things which ungodly sinners have spoken against Him."

The unbelievers on earth had their opportunity to accept the truth of Jesus, but they spurned the grace of God. Now, there is no more room for grace—only wrath.

## The Victory of the King

Revelation 19 closes with a powerful description of Jesus's victory over His enemies. John wrote, "And I saw the beast and the kings of the earth and their armies assembled to make war against Him who sat on the horse and against His army. And the beast was seized, and with him the false prophet who performed the signs in his presence, by which he deceived those who had received the mark of the beast and those who worshiped his image; these two were thrown alive into the lake of fire which burns with brimstone" (vv. 19–20).

This is the scene Jesus talked about in Matthew 24:30: "And then the sign of the Son of Man will appear in the sky, and then all the tribes of the earth will mourn, and they will see the Son of Man coming on the clouds of the sky with power and great glory."

The second coming of Jesus Christ will be the worst day of your life if you have to face Him as your Judge. But the second coming of Jesus Christ will be the best day of your life if you receive His forgiveness now and look forward to the great future He has planned for you.

# Nine Differences between the Rapture and Second Coming

Some Christians believe that the rapture of the church and the second coming of Jesus Christ are the same event, because the Bible uses the same Greek words to describe both events:

- *Parousia*—which means "coming," "arrival," or "presence" (1 Thessalonians 4:15; Matthew 24:27)

- *Apokalupsis*—which means "unveiling," "uncovering," or "revelation" (1 Corinthians 1:7; 2 Thessalonians 1:7)

- *Epiphaneia*—which means "manifestation" (2 Timothy 4:8; 2 Thessalonians 2:8).

If the Bible uses these same three words to describe both the rapture and the second coming, then isn't it natural to assume that these are the same event?

My friend and seminary professor Charles Ryrie reminded us that just because things are similar does not mean they are identical. For example, my car has a motor, my washing machine has a motor, and my garage door opener has a motor. But are these three items identical? Of course not.

Similarly, just because the rapture and the second coming of Christ are similar in some respects does not mean they are the same event. Suppose, Dr. Ryrie theorized, that some proud grandparents said to their friends, "We are looking forward to the coming of our grandchildren next week," and then later in the conversation they said, "We are excited that our grandchildren will be coming for our golden wedding anniversary." From those two statements, you could assume that (a) the grandparents are saying that their anniversary is next week and, thus, are speaking of their grandchildren's arrival and their anniversary as a single event; or (b) the grandparents are referring to two different events—the grandchildren are coming next week for a visit, but they will also be returning at a later time for the anniversary celebration. The two events are similar in many ways, but no one would argue they are the same event.

The same truth applies to the rapture and the second coming of Christ. In both events there will be a coming of the Lord from heaven (*parousia*), a revealing of His glory as the Son of God (*apokalupsis*), and a visible manifestation of Himself (*epiphaneia*).

But there are also at least nine major differences between the rapture and the second coming, which help us understand that they are two separate events.

Let's look briefly at each of these differences:

1. Many prophecies must be fulfilled prior to the second coming of Christ, including the return of Israel to her homeland, the rebuilding of the temple in Jerusalem, and the events of the tribulation described in Revelation. However, no prophecies must be fulfilled before the rapture of the church occurs. At any moment, the trumpet could sound, and believers could be caught up to meet the Lord in the air (1 Thessalonians 4:16–17). That is why we say that the rapture is imminent—it could happen at any moment.

2. At the rapture, Christ's feet never touch the earth. Instead, He appears to meet believers "in the air" (1 Thessalonians 4:17). But at the second coming, the Lord's feet will touch the earth, and when they do, what a topological reaction there will be! Not long ago, I stood on the Mount of Olives and read to our tour group this verse, which describes what will happen at the second coming: "In that day His feet will stand on the Mount of Olives, which is in front of

Jerusalem on the east; and the Mount of Olives will be split in its middle from east to west by a very large valley, so that half of the mountain will move toward the north and the other half toward the south" (Zechariah 14:4). When Jesus returns, the Mount of Olives will split in two!

3. At the rapture, Jesus will return to heaven with His believers. But at the second coming, Jesus will return to earth with believers to establish His kingdom.

4. The rapture is a mystery that is not mentioned in the Old Testament and involves only the church. But the second coming is predicted many times in the Old Testament since it involves God's program for Israel, the church, and the world.

5. After the rapture, believers will be judged at the judgment seat of Christ. The result of this judgment determines believers' rewards in heaven. After the second coming, unbelievers will be judged at the great white throne judgment. This is the final judgment of all unbelievers at the end of time.

6. After the rapture, there is no physical change in the earth. But after the second coming, part of the curse against the earth is removed, and the planet will enjoy a partial renovation.

7. After the rapture, Satan runs rampant on the earth for seven years. After the second coming, Satan is bound for one thousand years.

8. The rapture will occur instantaneously ("in the twinkling of an eye," as 1 Corinthians 15:52 says). The second coming will be the climax of a seven-year-long worldwide conflict involving millions of people.

9. Finally, at the rapture, only believers will see the Lord Jesus Christ. But at the second coming, unbelievers will "look on [Him] whom they have pierced" (Zechariah 12:10) and "every knee will bow, of those who are in heaven and on earth and under the earth, and that every tongue will confess that Jesus Christ is Lord, to the glory of God the Father" (Philippians 2:10–11).

## What Difference Do These Events Make?

What difference does it make if Jesus is literally coming back to the world one day, first in the rapture of the church and then, at the end of the tribulation seven years later, at His second coming?

I remember reading a story about a group of seminary students who were playing basketball. After they finished their basketball game, they headed to the shower, and one of the seminary students noticed a janitor sitting on the bleachers waiting for them to finish so he could clean up. As the seminary student walked past the janitor, he saw that the man was reading a Bible. So he asked, "What are you reading?" The janitor said, "I'm reading the book of Revelation." The seminary student knew how complicated the book of Revelation was, so he asked the janitor, "Do you understand what it means?" The janitor looked up and said, "Yes, sir. I understand what it means. It means Jesus is going to win."

One day Jesus is going to win, but let's be honest: As we look at the world today, it doesn't look like Jesus is winning, does it? We look around and see a world that's filled with sadness, with disease, with broken relationships, and with death. What we feel and what we see is real, but it's also temporary. The Bible says

one day Jesus is going to win. One day Jesus is coming back again to reclaim and re-create that which has been lost.

The apostle John looked forward to that day. He saw it before him in Revelation 11:15. He said, "Then the seventh angel sounded; and there were loud voices in heaven, saying, 'The kingdom of the world has now become the kingdom of our Lord and of His Christ; and He will reign forever and ever.'" Amen.

What's the practical application for us of the rapture of the church and the second coming of Christ? In Titus 2:13, Paul encouraged us to be looking for that blessed hope, the appearing of our great God, Jesus Christ. We are to live our lives in anticipation of the sure and certain coming of Christ.

Now, that doesn't mean we should quit our jobs, max out our credit cards, and go to Disney World. But it does mean that we ought to live our lives with the knowledge that at any moment, the trumpet could sound, the clouds could part, and the Lord Jesus Christ could appear to take us home. All we're waiting for right now is that trumpet blast before we are snatched away into the presence of our Lord Jesus Christ. Are you ready?[2]

# 6

# Why Has God Delayed the End Times?

One question I'm often asked—and perhaps you've been asked as well—is this: "Why is the Lord so slow in returning? We've heard this refrain for two thousand years that Jesus is coming back. But He hasn't come back yet. Why is He waiting? With the world situation like it is, why doesn't the Lord put an end to it and come back?"

Well, the apostle Peter faced that same question, and he answered it in 2 Peter 3:3–13. I want you to look at these verses very carefully. Peter warned,

> Know this first of all, that in the last days mockers will come with their mocking, following after their own lusts, and saying, "Where is the promise of His coming? For ever since the fathers fell asleep, all continues just as it was from the beginning

of creation." For when they maintain this, it escapes their notice that by the word of God the heavens existed long ago and the earth was formed out of water and by water, through which the world at that time was destroyed, being flooded with water. But by His word the present heavens and earth are being reserved for fire, kept for the day of judgment and destruction of ungodly men.

But do not let this one fact escape your notice, beloved, that with the Lord one day is like a thousand years, and a thousand years like one day. The Lord is not slow about His promise, as some count slowness, but is patient toward you, not wishing for any to perish but for all to come to repentance.

But the day of the Lord will come like a thief, in which the heavens will pass away with a roar and the elements will be destroyed with intense heat, and the earth and its works will be burned up.

Since all these things are to be destroyed in this way, what sort of people ought you to be in holy conduct and godliness, looking for and hastening the coming of the day of

God, because of which the heavens will be destroyed by burning, and the elements will melt with intense heat! But according to His promise we are looking for new heavens and a new earth, in which righteousness dwells.

Notice that in Matthew 24:36, Jesus said no one knows the day or the hour, but we also read in 2 Peter 3:12 that we are to be looking for and hastening the coming day of the Lord. So how close are we?

# Where Are We on God's Timetable?

That brings us to an all-important question: Where exactly are we on God's timetable? How close are we to the end? There are two places we need to look to answer that question.

## Look at the World Situation

First of all, we need to look at the world situation. That's one way to know how close we are. And when I talk about the world situation, I'm talking specifically about the Middle East, and, even more specifically, Israel. The Bible says the final world events before the return of Christ that matter won't be occurring in London, New York, or Tokyo; the final events that usher in the return of Christ will take place in Israel

and the nations around Israel. Now, again, we can't know the hour or day, but I want you to notice these four truths about the world situation.

Number one, there is a clear pattern of events laid out in the Bible concerning the last days. When you tie together the Old Testament and the New Testament, there is a clear pattern about what's going to happen immediately before Christ returns. Specifically, there is going to be increased hostility toward the Jewish people and toward the nation of Israel, and there's going to be intense hatred for Christians. Those two things go hand in hand. The Antichrist will launch a campaign of persecution against the Jews and against believers. There will be an intense hatred of Israel that will result in an invasion of Israel. You can see that happening right now. You can see nation after nation turning its back on Israel. You can see in the United States of America a vocal segment of the population that is aggressively anti-Israel and anti-semitic. I think, personally, all it's going to take is a couple of major terrorist events in this country that are tied to those groups that hate Israel for most Americans to say it's time to bail out in our support for Israel. We're only about a couple of events away from that happening. That is a sign of the end.

Number two, there is an amazing similarity between our world and the world the Bible describes at the end of time. In Matthew 24–25, Jesus laid out what is going to happen in the world before He returns. And yes, it's true that a lot of those signs have been around for a long time. But, as Jesus said, those signs are going to be like the labor pains a woman experiences before birth. They are going to increase in both frequency and intensity, and we're seeing that happen in our world today.

Number three, if that is true, then we indeed may be the generation to experience the rapture of the church. Remember, the rapture occurs seven years before the second coming. If the second coming is close, how much closer will be the rapture of the church? I read that Anne Graham Lotz, the daughter of Billy Graham, said she believes she will be alive to see the rapture of the church.[1] She may or may not be right about that, but the rapture is getting closer every day. And as I've said so often, one of two things is certain: either He's coming, or we're going. But we're living in the last days for all of us.

Number four, every sign points in one direction: our confrontation with God is coming. It's nearer today than it's ever been.

## Look at the Bible

Second, in order to understand where we are on God's

timetable, we need to look at the Bible. Why is the Lord slow in His coming? Remember what Peter said: "The Lord is not slow about His promise, as some count slowness, but is patient toward you, not wishing for any to perish but for all to come to repentance. But the day of the Lord will come like a thief, in which the heavens will pass away with a roar and the elements will be destroyed with intense heat, and the earth and its works will be burned up" (2 Peter 3:9–10).

Here are three important insights from this passage about the second coming of Christ.

Number one, the Lord's return is certain because God promised it. We have the same scoffers today that were present in Peter's day. These people say, "Where is the promise of His coming? You talk about it all the time, but I don't see Him anywhere."

I'll never forget the time I was listening to a popular preacher on the radio on Easter Sunday morning, and he said, "Oh, all these Christians looking for the coming of Jesus. Why, people have been saying for centuries that Jesus is coming back. He hasn't come back yet, and He's not coming back." I couldn't believe he was saying such a thing. But that's what scoffers will say in the last days.

In Matthew 24:37–39, Jesus pointed out that there was another time when people were scoffing at God's promise—right before the flood. God had promised to destroy the world because of its wickedness, but the flood was delayed. People scoffed at the idea, but one day, as Jesus said, while they were eating, drinking, marrying, and giving in marriage, the flood came and swept them all away. So will it be when Christ returns. The Lord's return is certain because Jesus has promised it.

Number two, the Lord's return will usher in a day of judgment for the ungodly. When the flood "came and took them all away," it swept unbelievers away into everlasting judgment (v. 39). God destroyed the world once with water, and He promised He would never do it again. Every time you see a rainbow, that is God's promise that He won't destroy the world by water (Genesis 9:11–17). But 2 Peter 3:7 says He is going to destroy it by fire. When the Lord returns, everything we see is going to be burned up. That is going to be good news for those of us who are believers. But it is terrible news for unbelievers because the Lord's return signals His judgment.

Number three, the Lord's return is delayed to give people a chance to trust in Christ. The scoffers ask, "Where is the promise of His coming?" They don't understand that this delay is for their benefit. God has delayed His judgment to give unbelievers one final chance to repent. You see, God does not hate people; He loves people. But He's also a God of justice. He must judge sin. God has provided a way of escape through faith in Jesus Christ, and God is giving every person one last chance to repent before judgment day comes.

# 7

# How Do I Prepare for the End Times?

As we have seen, the rapture is the next event on God's prophetic timeline, and it could happen at any time—perhaps before you finish reading this chapter. How does the certainty of an imminent future rapture affect our lives today?

A biblical understanding of the end times should lead us to trust in Christ for our salvation so that we can escape the reality of hell and experience eternal life with God in the new heaven and new earth. But understanding the end times should also affect the way we live whatever brief time we have left in this life.

In Titus 2:13, the apostle Paul encouraged Titus to be "looking for the blessed hope and the appearing of the glory of our great God and Savior, Christ Jesus." In other words, we should live in expectation that at any moment the rapture could occur. Paul spoke of the imminence of the rapture in 1 Corinthians 15:52:

"In a moment, in the twinkling of an eye, at the last trumpet; for the trumpet will sound, and the dead will be raised imperishable, and we will be changed."

Although there are numerous prophecies that need to be fulfilled before the second coming, there are no prophecies that must be fulfilled prior to the rapture. It could happen next year, next week, or before you finish reading this paragraph. We should live each day with the realization that at any time the trumpet could sound, and the Lord could appear for His own.

God's Word reminds us that we need to live as "aliens and strangers" (1 Peter 2:11) in this world, which is about to be destroyed. It tells us to "be of sober spirit" and "be on the alert" for His appearance (5:8). All we are waiting for is the sound of the trumpet, at which time Jesus will appear and snatch us away to be with Him in heaven forever.

Until that time, Jesus calls us to be salt and light in our nation and world (Matthew 5:13–16). Although we can't prevent the ultimate destruction of the world, we can postpone it. We have both the ability and responsibility to delay the decay of our nation, even if we can't ultimately reverse it. Why should we work to postpone the inevitable? The same reason we exercise, take medicine, and watch our diets. While those efforts can't prevent our ultimate demise, such actions can delay it!

The motivation for Christians working to delay the coming collapse of our world is not to preserve our way of life but to buy more time to share the life-changing gospel of Jesus Christ with as many people as possible before they are swept away by God's judgment.

The Bible never divorces prophetic truth from practical application. In 2 Peter 3, the apostle described the return of Christ, the destruction of the earth, and the creation of the new heaven and earth. Then he added these words: "Since all these things are to be destroyed in this way, what sort of people ought you to be in holy conduct and godliness, looking for and hastening the coming of the day of God" (vv. 11–12). One way we prepare for the day of the Lord is by spreading the gospel to everyone on earth (Matthew 24:14).

In his book *World Aflame*, Billy Graham told of an incident when President Dwight Eisenhower was vacationing in Denver. Eisenhower read an open letter in a local newspaper from six-year-old Paul Haley, dying of cancer, who wished to see the president of the United States. In a spontaneous, gracious gesture, the president decided to grant the boy's request.

One Sunday morning, a limousine pulled up outside the Haley home, and out stepped President Eisenhower. The president knocked at the door, and Donald Haley, the boy's father, opened it. He was wearing blue jeans, an old shirt, and a day's growth of beard. Behind him was little Paul. They were amazed to see the president of the United States on their doorstep!

"Paul," said the president, "I'm glad to see you." He shook Paul's hand, and the two walked together and conversed for a while. They shook hands again, and the president departed.

President Eisenhower's kind and thoughtful deed was talked about for many years afterward. Only one person was not entirely happy about it—Mr. Haley. He could never forget how he was dressed when he opened the door. "Old jeans, that faded shirt, my unshaven face. What a way to greet the president of the United States," he lamented.[1]

I can tell you something even more embarrassing than that. One day, the Bible says, the trumpet will sound, the heavens will part, and we will see the King of kings and Lord of lords. When that happens, tragically, many Christians will be embarrassed by their lives. They will be clothed in immorality, greed, and personal ambition instead of being clothed in the righteous acts of the saints.

Let me ask you this: When you meet God face-to-face, either through your death or through the rapture, will you be embarrassed about the life you have lived up to this point? If so, now is the time to make those changes that will ensure you are ready for your coming appointment with God.

I pray that this brief study of the end times will be a powerful incentive for you to clothe yourself in "holy conduct and godliness" (2 Peter 3:11) as we look forward to His certain return.

God has given you and me the ability right now to make changes in our lives that can change how those end-times events affect us. Right now, we can examine whether we're truly saved, whether we're focused on the things of God, and how we can make changes in those areas that will impact our eternity.

## Awaiting the Return of Jesus Christ

The end-times events are set. We're not going to change that, but how we respond right now will determine whether these events are a prelude to an eternity of blessing or to a nightmare like we've never known. In John 16:33, Jesus said to His disciples, "In the world you have tribulation, but take courage; I have overcome the world." And so will everyone who belongs to Jesus Christ.

The Bible says two things about the return of Jesus to give us hope as we await His coming.

## His Coming Is Certain

First of all, Jesus's coming is certain. In John 14:3, Jesus made this promise: "If I go and prepare a place for you, I will come again and receive you to Myself, that where I am, there you may be also."

Jesus promised, "I will come again." And we see that promise about the Lord's triumphant return throughout the Bible. Did you know in the New Testament alone there are over three hundred verses that talk about the return of Jesus? One out of every thirteen verses in the New Testament has something to do with the Lord's return. And although Christians differ on some of the minute details of His return, the constant refrain from the beginning of Christianity has been that Jesus is coming again.

In Acts 1, we see that certainty about the Lord's return. At this time, Jesus had been on the earth forty days after His resurrection. He was in His new body, and thousands of people saw Him. Finally, He assembled with His followers on the Mount of Olives, and He ascended into the heavens. Can you imagine

117

what that scene was like as the disciples looked up and saw the Lord lifted up into heaven? And as the disciples were gazing into heaven, two angels said to them in Acts 1:11, "Men of Galilee, why do you stand looking into the sky?" Of course they were looking into the sky! Who wouldn't be after such a miraculous event? But the angels continued, "This Jesus, who has been taken up from you into heaven, will come in just the same way as you have watched Him go into heaven" (v. 11). The angels were saying, "This same Jesus, the one you've been with for these last three years, is going to come back from heaven the same way He just went up into heaven."

How did Jesus go up into heaven? Did He go figuratively into heaven? No, His body ascended into heaven. Jesus went up literally, visibly, and bodily into heaven. And the angels said He is going to return the same way. I've heard preachers on the radio say things like, "Oh, Jesus is coming back again. His second coming is when He comes into your heart." That's what some people believe: the second coming of Jesus is when He comes into your heart. But the angels said that Jesus is coming back literally, visibly, and bodily, for everyone to see. That's the promise of Scripture. His coming is certain.

## His Coming Is Soon

Second, the Bible promises His coming is soon. How can I say that with such certainty? Remember, there are no prophecies that have to be fulfilled before the rapture takes place. The rapture is imminent. It could happen before you finish reading this book. So in that sense, His coming is soon.

Think about it this way: If two thousand years ago the apostles were talking about the soon coming of the Lord, how much closer is His coming today than it was then? Paul alluded to that in Romans 13:11–12. The apostle Paul believed the Lord was coming soon. Look at what he said: "Do this, knowing the time, that it is already the hour for you to awaken from sleep; for now salvation is nearer to us than when we believed. The night is almost gone, and the day is near." Paul had done the math in his head. He had figured out that the coming of the Lord was closer, and it's easy to see why he believed that. If there is a date fixed on God's calendar when Christ is coming back again, then every second that passes moves us closer to that day. So Paul was saying that our salvation—meaning our deliverance out of this sin-infected world that will occur when Christ returns—is nearer to us today than when we believed a few years ago. Time is passing. It is moving us toward that soon return of Jesus Christ.

Imagine the apostle Paul were writing to us today. What would he say to us? He would say, "Wake up! Remove the sleep from your eyes. If I thought the Lord's return was close when I wrote to the Romans two thousand years ago, then how much closer is it today? The Lord's return is near. He is coming soon."

As we await Jesus's return, we're to live expectantly, knowing what time it is. I once read a story about a family that had grandfather clock. The clock would chime every hour: at one o'clock, it would chime once, at two o'clock, it would chime twice, and so on. One night in the wee hours, the grandfather clock malfunctioned and chimed thirteen times. The little boy in the house awakened, and he ran through the house, yelling, "Get up! Get up, everybody! It's later than it's ever been!"[2] That's what Paul was saying to us: "Wake up! We are closer today to the Lord's coming than we have ever been." The Lord's coming is certain, and the Lord's coming will be soon.

## How to Live in These Last Days

How are we to live in light of the certain and soon coming of the Lord? As we look through Scripture, we find four qualities that ought to characterize every believer who is living in these last days.

## People of Hope

First of all, the Bible says we are to be people of hope. It's easy to look at the world situation today and get discouraged: we see escalating conflicts in the Middle East, Russia's invasion of Ukraine, increasing tensions with China, and the possibility of a nuclear Iran. There are many reasons to be concerned about the world situation.

Not long ago, former defense secretary Chuck Hagel spoke at the Washington Ideas Festival. He wasn't sanguine about the future of the world. He said, "I think we are living through one of these historic defining times. We are seeing a new world order—post-World War II, post-Soviet Union implosion—being built. . . . Tyranny, terrorism . . . is going to be with us. It's a reality. I see these things continuing."[3] In other words, get used to the world situation. It's going to continue; it is only going to get worse.

So how can we be people of hope given what's happening in the world today? Our hope does not rest in Washington, DC. Our hope is not found in any politician. Look at what the psalmist said: "And now, Lord, for what do I wait? My hope is in You" (Psalm 39:7). Our hope is in the everlasting God.

Romans 15:13 contains one of the most beautiful benedictions found in Scripture. Paul closed his letter to the Christians in Rome with these words: "Now may the God of hope fill you with all joy and peace in believing, so that you will abound in hope by the power of the Holy Spirit." Do you see the repetition of "hope" in that prayer? We serve the God of hope, and because of that we ought to abound in hope ourselves. That Greek word translated "abound" refers to a river that overflows its banks. Paul was saying that our lives ought to be like a river overflowing with hope. That is, we ought to be so full of hope that when people get close to us, they can't help but get splashed by the hope of God.

If we're constantly discouraged and fearful, what kind of witness is that? What kind of message does that send to unbelievers? Instead, the apostle Peter said, "Always [be] ready to make a defense to everyone who asks you to give an account for the hope that is in you" (1 Peter 3:15). Notice that he didn't say "the doom and gloom that is in you" or "the despair that is in you" or "the discouragement that is in you." No, he said, "Always [be] ready to make a defense to everyone who asks you to give an account for the *hope* that is in you." Christians ought to be hopeful, optimistic people. In these last days, we ought to be overflowing with hope.

## People of Insight

Second, the Bible says that as we live in these last days, we are to be people of insight. Tucked away in 1 Chronicles 12 is the verse I think best describes how we ought to be living in times like these. This passage lists the Jewish men who decided to leave the service of King Saul and join forces with David, God's man, at Hebron. The writer divided these men by tribe: those from Judah, Levi, Benjamin, Ephraim, and so on. But when the writer listed the men from the tribe of Issachar, he added these words: "The sons of Issachar, men who understood the times, with knowledge of what Israel should do" (v. 32).

The sons of Issachar understood the times. They knew what was happening in their nation. The sons of Issachar knew there was a shift in the political winds. They understood the moral and spiritual climate of their nation. And we need to be the same way today. We need to have our finger on the pulse of what is happening in this country and what is happening in this world—morally, spiritually, and politically.

Some Christians say, "Oh, I don't get involved in current events. I don't keep up with the news; it's too depressing. I just read my Bible. It's just me and God. I let other people handle all that stuff." That's not being a godly person; that's being an ignorant person. And God places no premium on ignorance. You don't get any brownie points in heaven by being ignorant about what's happening in the world. God says if you're going to be a godly person, you need to understand the times in which God has placed you. That's what the sons of Issachar did. They understood the times.

## People of Action

Third, in these last days, we are to be people of action. Notice that in 1 Chronicles 12:32, the sons of Issachar knew what the people of God should do. The reason they sought to understand what was happening in their country was so that they would know what they should *do*. Based on the knowledge they obtained, they took action. They concluded that it was time to shift their allegiance away from King Saul and to follow God's man, David.

It's easy for us to get discouraged in the world today and talk about what terrible times we're living in. I think about Catholic theologian Richard John Neuhaus. He had traveled for a speaking engagement in another city, and the host arrived to pick him up at the airport. As they drove to the speaking event, the driver lamented over and over about what terrible times they were living in. Father Neuhaus finally had enough, and he said, "The times may be bad, but they are the only times we are given. Remember, hope is still a Christian virtue, and despair is a mortal sin."[4] That's what the sons of Issachar said: "Yes, the times are terrible, but these are the times in which we are living, and we ought to do something." People of insight are people who not only understand their times but also know what they should do.

In these last days, we are to be people of action, not just hunkering down or sitting around waiting for the end to come. We're to be people who are doing something. Not long ago, I read about a well-known evangelical pastor who was talking to a group of pastors about what we ought to be doing. And he said some good things. He talked about Christians' need to live out our faith daily. He said that if Christians would stop watching pornography, if we would stop gossiping and slandering, if we would start living true to our faith, we could make a difference in this world. And I agree with that 100 percent. But then he said something that could not have been more wrong. He said that he thought Christians needed to take a year off from the culture wars and just concentrate on their own relationship with God. Take a year off? Take a year off from fighting for the sanctity of life when a million babies are being murdered every year? Take a year off from speaking out against immorality when the sanctity of marriage is coming under attack? Take a year off from speaking out against human trafficking and other atrocities that are taking place in the world?

If we want to be like the sons of Issachar, we don't get to take time off. We will always be involved in doing God's work. And make no mistake about it: God has called us to confront an evil society. He's called us to confront evil leaders. He's called us to confront all immorality and say without stuttering or stammering, "Thus sayeth the Lord." We are to be actively involved in influencing our culture.

In Matthew 5:13, Jesus said to His disciples, "You are the salt of the earth; but if the salt has become tasteless, how can it be made salty again? It is no longer good for anything, except to be thrown out and trampled under foot by men." When Jesus talked about being salt, He was talking about being a preservative. That's what salt did in Jesus's day. It didn't prevent the decaying of meat; it delayed the decay of meat. It gave the meat a longer shelf life until it eventually had to be thrown out. So Jesus was saying, "As My representatives in the world today, you are to be a preservative in this culture; you are to keep this world from prematurely imploding so that people have longer to accept the gospel."

For salt to preserve meat, it can't remain in the

saltshaker. It has to get out of the shaker; it has to penetrate the meat itself. God has not called us to take off a year from engaging with our culture. He's called upon us to influence this world, to push back against the tide of immorality that is engulfing us. We are salt.

Jesus also said, "You are the light of the world. A city set on a hill cannot be hidden" (v. 14). At the same time that we are pushing back against evil, we are to be holding forth the light of the gospel. It's not either/or. Jesus didn't say, "You are salt *or* light." He said, "You are salt *and* light." We are to confront evil and share Jesus at the same time.

One of my favorite verses in the Bible is Daniel 11:32. It says, "The people who know their God will display strength and take action." God has called us not just to understand the times, but also to do something.

## People of Courage

Finally, we're to be people of courage. To be salt and light in today's world takes courage. A. W. Tozer once said, "A scared world needs a fearless church."[5] God wants us to be fearless people as we stand for Him.

Are you ready to stand for God and His truth regardless of the cost? Persecution is coming. It's coming—not just around the world but to this country as well. Are you ready for it? Sadly, most Christians aren't. If they just hear about the possibility of suffering or persecution, they run for the exits of the church. They hide under the bed. They're fearful of suffering. But Jesus told us to get ready; persecution is coming (Matthew 24:9). Are you ready to suffer for Christ?

And that leads to another question: How do we prepare for the certain and soon coming of the Lord? How can we be at peace with God, certain that our eternal future is secure?

## How Can We Be at Peace with God?

We look at the world around us and say, "What in the world is wrong with the world?" To answer that question, all you have to do is look in the mirror. What's wrong with the world? You're the problem. I'm the problem. The turmoil in the world today is because of a turmoil that exists in every human heart—a turmoil that is caused by sin, which is rebellion against God. The Bible says we've all sinned (Romans 3:23). We've all rebelled against God. And everything that is wrong in the world today can be traced back to that rebellion. We all are deserving of God's judgment.

How can we be made right with God? How can we be at peace with God? Look at what Paul said in

Romans 5:1: "Therefore, having been justified by faith, we have peace with God through our Lord Jesus Christ." The only way we can be at peace with God, the only way we can be assured of being welcomed into heaven, is to be justified by God. That word "justified" is a legal term. It means to be declared not guilty. The only hope any of us has is that we will be found not guilty before God. But here is the problem: we're all guilty before God. You don't need me to tell you that. You've sinned, I've sinned; we've all sinned. We're very, very guilty. How could God ever find us not guilty?

That is the miracle of the gospel of Jesus Christ. When Jesus died on the cross, He willingly took the punishment for your sin and my sin. And when we trust in Jesus for our salvation, in that great courtroom of heaven, God bangs the gavel down and says, "Not guilty. Justified. Freely forgiven forever."

The only hope we have to be at peace with God when He comes or when we go to be with Him and stand before Him in judgment, is to be found not guilty. That's the way we prepare for the certain and soon return of Christ.

There's an old fable about Satan meeting with three new apprentice demons. He told the demons that their job was to deceive people from turning to the truth and knowing Christ as Savior. So he said to the demons, "Now, how do you propose to deceive people?"

The first demon raised his hand and said, "I'll tell people there is no God." Satan said, "No, that won't work. Everybody can look around and know there has to be a God who created all this."

The second demon raised his hand and said, "I'll tell people there is no hell." Satan said, "That won't work either. Deep down, everybody knows there has to be a place of judgment for unbelievers and evildoers."

The third demon raised his hand and said, "I'll tell people there is no hurry." Satan smiled and said, "With that, you will deceive millions."

You may be thinking, *I know I need to get things right with God someday. I know things aren't what they should be, and I'll get around to it one day. But I've got my family responsibilities. I've got this problem at work. I've got this health issue I'm dealing with. I've got some living I want to do. I'll get around to it eventually. There's no hurry.*

That's the deception of Satan. The truth is, today is the only day you have. And today very well may be the last day you have. That's why Scripture says today is the day of salvation (2 Corinthians 6:2). Jesus is coming again. Are you ready?[6]

If you would like to be forgiven of your sins so you will be ready to meet the Lord, I invite you to pray this simple prayer, knowing that God will hear you and answer:

*Dear God, thank You for loving me. I know that I have failed You in so many ways, and I'm truly sorry for the sins in my life. But I believe that You love me so much You sent Your Son, Jesus, to die on the cross for my sins, to take the punishment that I deserve. And right now, I'm trusting not in my good works but in what Jesus did to save me from my sins. Thank You for forgiving me, and help me to spend the rest of my life following You. I pray this in Jesus's name.*

# Appendix A

# The Rise of Radical Islam

In 2014, a radio host asked a simple question: "Can we expect more beheadings in the United States?" The answer from Robert Spencer was equally direct: "Nothing is more certain than that."[1] Spencer knows what he's talking about. He's the president of Jihad Watch, an organization that watches the actions of Islamic terrorists around the world. He understands the connection between radical Islam and terrorism, and he predicts we're going to start seeing the violent activity of radical Islam in our own country as well.

In the years since Spencer's interview, his grim prediction of the rise of radical Islam in our world has proven to be alarmingly accurate. We've indeed witnessed a horrifying escalation of violence from Islamic terrorist groups, including not only beheadings but also atrocities like slaughtering entire families and setting homes on fire.

Who are the people committing these ghastly acts? What do they believe? What is their goal? And most importantly, what is their connection to the return of Jesus Christ?

# The Connection between Terrorism and Radical Islam

In chapter 3, we looked at five signs Jesus said would precede His visible, literal return to earth. Although Jesus made it clear in Matthew 24 that no man knows the day or hour of His return, we should know the signs that will lead to His return so that we can be alert and prepared. Remember, one of the signs Jesus described is international conflict. Throughout history, our world has experienced near-constant conflicts and wars. And much of the global violence today comes from terrorist groups rooted in radical Islam.

Is it fair to connect terrorism we've been seeing around the world with the so-called peaceful religion of Islam? Many leaders in the West say that's an unfair connection. They deny there is any relationship between these acts of terror and Islam. They are dead wrong in their assertion. All we have to do is listen to what these terrorists say about the motivation for their actions. These terror groups go by different names—such as ISIS, ISIL, the Islamic State, Islamic Jihad Organization, Hezbollah, and Hamas. But all those names are connected to the religion of Islam.

Make no mistake about it: these terrorists are doing what they are doing in the name of their Muslim faith. When they commit these acts of terror, they are doing what their book of faith, the Qur'an, commands them to do. They are not acting in opposition to their faith; they are obeying the tenets of their faith found in the Qur'an.

These militant Muslims take seriously the words of Surah 9:5, the famous "Sword Verse" in the Qur'an: "Then, when the sacred months have passed, slay the idolaters [that's you and me] wherever ye find them, and take them (captive), and besiege them, and prepare for them each ambush. But if they repent and establish worship and pay the poor-due, then leave their way free. Lo! Allah is Forgiving, Merciful." This verse isn't an aberration or taken out of context. It's one of numerous verses in the Qur'an that call for violence against what the Qur'an calls "the people of the book"—referring to Jews and Christians.

I'd like to pause here and point out an important difference between this and what the New Testament teaches. The New Testament is our guiding principle for how we live and behave. You cannot find one single verse in the New Testament that calls for violence against unbelievers. Jesus said to love your enemies. Muhammad said to slay your enemies. That's the difference between Islam and Christianity.

Why do radical Islamic terrorists commit horrific acts against Jews and Christians? They are doing it because their faith tells them to do it. They burn churches in the name of Allah. They kidnap in the name of Allah. They behead in the name of Allah. They commit murder in the name of Allah, strictly following the teachings of the Qur'an in their radical loyalty to Islam. They want to establish a worldwide Muslim caliphate and impose Sharia law.

When I speak on the subject of radical Islam on radio and television programs, people often point out, "But there are extreme Christians, too, who do horrible things in the name of their faith." That is true, and we have to acknowledge that. But when they do those things, they're acting in opposition to what the New Testament says. Remember, there is no verse in the New Testament that calls for violence against unbelievers.

I'll be the first to admit it would be unfair to say all Muslims are violent. As I mentioned in chapter 3, the most conservative estimate is that only 5 percent of Muslims today embrace the ideology of radical Islam. But there are 1.7 billion Muslims in the world. If only 5 percent embrace radical Islam, that is eighty-five million Muslims in the world who believe in the use of force to achieve their goal.[2] That should alarm everyone.

I agree with the words of Israeli prime minister

Benjamin Netanyahu when he acknowledged that while these radical Islamic terrorist groups are different in many ways, they are all anti-Israel, anti-West, and in favor of using violence to achieve their goals. Speaking to the United Nations, Netanyahu framed the issue like this: "Militant Islam's ambition to dominate the world seems mad. But so too did the global ambitions of another fanatic ideology that swept to power eight decades ago. The Nazis believed in a master race. The militant Islamists believe in a master faith. They just disagree about who among them will be the master . . . of the master faith. That's what they truly disagree about. Therefore, the question before us is whether militant Islam will have the power to realize its unbridled ambitions."[3]

What is the origin of Islam? What is its goal, and how does it fit within Bible prophecy? Let's look at God's Word to answer those questions.

# The Origin of Islam

Contrary to what you may have been taught, Islam did not originate fourteen hundred years ago with a man named Muhammad. It began four thousand years ago with a man named Abraham.

## The Abrahamic Covenant

As we saw in chapter 2, Abraham was a wealthy man who lived in Ur of the Chaldeans, a metropolitan city located in what is now southern Iraq, close to the Persian Gulf. In Genesis 12, God appeared to Abraham and said this:

> Go forth from your country,
>
> And from your relatives
>
> And from your father's house,
>
> To the land which I will show you;
>
> And I will make you a great nation,
>
> And I will bless you,
>
> And make your name great;
>
> And so you shall be a blessing;
>
> And I will bless those who bless you,
>
> And the one who curses you I will curse.
>
> And in you all the families of the earth will be blessed. (vv. 1–3)

These verses are known as the Abrahamic covenant, which is key to understanding history from the rest of the book of Genesis until the second coming of Christ in Revelation. As we have seen,

God's promise to Abraham and his descendants was literal, eternal, and unconditional.

The big question is this: Through which of Abraham's descendants would this blessing be passed?

## Hagar and Ishmael

Ten years after God made this promise to Abraham, Abraham was eighty-five years old—and still childless. So Abraham and Sarah decided to take matters into their own hands. They concocted a plan whereby Abraham would have a son through Hagar, the handmaid of Sarah.

This was a terrible idea, but Abraham went along with it and had sexual relations with Hagar. When Hagar became pregnant, there was tension between Hagar and Sarah. Finally, Hagar couldn't take the mistreatment from Sarah any longer, so she fled into the desert.

Now, it's important to understand that God didn't hate Hagar. He loved Hagar, and He loved Hagar's descendants.

While Hagar was in the desert, the angel of the Lord appeared to her and told her to return to Sarah. Then the angel gave her two astounding promises. The first promise was this: "I will greatly multiply your descendants so that they will be too many to count"

(Genesis 16:10). Just as God had promised that Abraham would be the father of a great nation, He said Hagar would be the mother of a vast multitude. "The angel of the LORD said to her further, 'Behold, you are with child, and you will bear a son; and you shall call his name Ishmael [meaning "God hears"]; because the LORD has given heed to your affliction'" (v. 11).

In verse 12, the angel made this prophecy about Hagar's son Ishmael and his descendants: "He will be a wild donkey of a man." That may sound insulting in our way of thinking, but this phrase wasn't an insult in Abraham's day. It simply meant that Ishmael and his descendants would be fiercely independent.

Next, the angel said, "His hand will be against everyone, and everyone's hand will be against him" (v. 12). In other words, Ishmael and his descendants were going to be in conflict with everyone around them.

Finally, the angel said, "And he will live to the east of all his brothers" (v. 12). Who are "his brothers"? This refers to the other descendants of Abraham who would come, including the Jewish people. Remember, Abraham was living in Canaan, which is the land where Israel is located today. God said the descendants of Ishmael would live to the east of Israel.

Thirteen years after Ishmael was born, God

appeared to Abraham and reminded him of His promise to make Abraham's descendants into a great nation. Since Ishmael was Abraham's only son at the time, he blurted out: "Oh that Ishmael might live before you!" (17:18). Abraham was saying, "God, You've already fulfilled Your promise. Ishmael's the one, isn't he?" But God said no. In verse 19, God said, "No, but Sarah your wife will bear you a son, and you shall call his name Isaac; and I will establish My covenant with him for an everlasting covenant for his descendants after him."

God said very clearly, "No, it's not Ishmael. I'm going to bless Ishmael and his descendants, but the covenant I made with you when you were seventy-five—My promise of a land, nation, and blessing—will go through a child you will have with your wife, Sarah."

When Abraham was ninety-nine and Sarah was eighty-nine, a great miracle occurred when Sarah became pregnant with Abraham's son Isaac.

## Abraham and Radical Islam

What does God's promise to Abraham four thousand years ago have to do with the recent rise of radical Islam? To this day, there are essentially two lines in the Middle East—the descendants of Isaac and the descendants of Ishmael. The *Nelson Study Bible* explains, "Ishmael's descendants are the Arab peoples who populate most of the Middle East today. Very few of the peoples of the Old Testament world have survived to our own day. . . . But two peoples survive: Israel, the Jewish Israel, the Jewish people, descended from Isaac, and the Arabs, descended from Ishmael."[4] Jews claim to be Abraham's descendants through Isaac, while Muslims believe they're Abraham's descendants through Ishmael. Ishmael is the spiritual father of the Arab people and, ultimately, of the Muslim faith. There is not a Muslim today who doesn't claim in some way to be linked to Ishmael.

And that brings us to our current situation. Muslims cannot accept the fact that the covenant God made to Abraham went through Isaac, not through Ishmael, so the land that God promised Abraham and his descendants rightfully belongs to the descendants of Isaac, not to the descendants of Ishmael. That was the decree of almighty God.

So the Muslims rewrote Scripture. They came up with a fanciful story about Abraham and Hagar taking Ishmael and fleeing to Mecca. There, these Muslims say, Ishmael became the forerunner of Muhammad—and thus all Muslims. In addition, Muslims don't accept the Bible's account of God's blessing going through Abraham and Isaac (Genesis 17:19). Instead, they claim the Jews just wrote that in there; the blessing really went through Abraham and Ishmael. They also take the story of Genesis 22—when Abraham took Isaac up on Mount Moriah to offer him as a sacrifice—and they say it was Ishmael, not Isaac, who was offered on Mount Moriah. They completely fabricate a story in order to make their point.

Now, remember, God did promise to bless Ishmael and his descendants. Genesis 17:20 says, "As for Ishmael, I have heard you; behold, I will bless him, and will make him fruitful and will multiply him exceedingly. He shall become the father of twelve princes, and I will make him a great nation." Has God blessed Ishmael and his descendants? Think of all the oil and resources in the Middle East. You better believe He has blessed the Arab people just as He said He would. But God said the Abrahamic covenant is not theirs. It belongs to Abraham through Isaac and his descendants.

In Genesis 17:21, God said, "My covenant I will establish with Isaac, whom Sarah will bear to you at this season next year." Regardless of what any negotiations accomplish or what any United Nations resolution says, the Bible makes it clear that the land of Israel belongs to the Jewish people. It is theirs by the decree of almighty God. The clashes we see today between Israel and many Arab nations are rooted in this conflict that began four thousand years ago about who owns the land.

Did you know that the most contested piece of real estate on planet Earth is the Temple Mount in Jerusalem? This is where the temple stood before it was destroyed in AD 70 by the Romans. When you go up to the Temple Mount today, in the place of a temple you find the Dome of the Rock—a holy site for the Muslims. The Arabs don't want any Jews on that mount, and the Jews don't want any Arabs. Today, there are soldiers walking around with machine guns, and there are little skirmishes from time to time. Sometimes people are killed up there because the Jews believe that land and that place belongs to them. And the Bible says one day, the Dome of the Rock is coming down, and a temple is going to be rebuilt there that will precede the return of Jesus Christ.

This is speculation, but I believe that an effort to rebuild the temple could be the catalyst that triggers the final world conflict that eventually leads to Armageddon. The fact is, there is no more contested place of real estate in the world right now than the Temple Mount.

# The Goal of Islam

Despite the differences in various sects of Islam, all of radical Islam is united in this: they hate Jews, they hate Christians, they hate anyone in the West who supports Jews or Christians, and they even hate moderate Muslims who won't support them. They are determined not only to evacuate Jews from the land of Israel but also to exterminate every Jew and Christian from the face of the earth and establish a worldwide Muslim caliphate. And they are dedicated to using whatever means necessary to achieve that goal.

Now, that brings up an interesting point. People ask me, "Isn't Islam just another way to approach God? Don't we all worship the same God, and we just call Him by different names?" I realize it is not popular to say this, but the God of the Bible is not Allah of the Qur'an. The Jesus of the Bible is not the Jesus of the Qur'an. Christians do not believe the same things as Muslims or worship the same God.

Let me say this without any hesitation: Islam is a false religion that is based on a false book that was written by a false prophet.

First, Islam is a false religion. If you sincerely follow the tenets of Islam with all your heart, when you die you will end up in hell, not in heaven. Islam does not lead a person to the true God. It leads people away from the true God. It is a false religion.

Second, Islam is based on a false book. The Qur'an was written by one person, Muhammad, over a period of twenty years. But there is not one single prophecy in the Qur'an that has ever been fulfilled. There is not one piece of archeological evidence to confirm anything in the Qur'an. It is an absolutely false book.

Muhammad claimed that an angel appeared to him and delivered to him the Muslim faith that is found in the Qur'an. Now, I believe an angel did appear to him. In Galatians 1:8, Paul said, "Even if we, *or an angel from heaven*, should preach to you a gospel contrary to what we have preached to you, he is to be accursed!" And 2 Corinthians 11:14 says, "Satan disguises himself as an angel of light." I believe the angel that Muhammad saw was Satan himself, who disguised himself as an angel of light and delivered this delusion to lead millions of people away from the one true God.

Third, Islam comes from a false prophet. Muhammad was not a man of God. He was a warlord who butchered God's people. He beheaded six hundred Jews because they wouldn't follow him into battle. So when we see radical Islamic terrorists beheading people today, they are simply following the example of the forerunner of their faith, Muhammad.

Now, when I talk about Islam, people often say, "Don't you know you will turn Muslims off to Christianity if you deride their prophet and their holy book, the Qur'an?" The fact is, if you really are concerned about the eternal destiny of Muslims, then you won't sugarcoat the truth to make yourself more acceptable to Muslims. If you really care about Muslims, you will tell them the truth—that their religion is based on a fraud. There is only one way to God, and it is through His Son, the Lord Jesus Christ. Remember, God loves Muslims just as much as He loves you and me. And the most loving thing we can do for Muslims is to introduce them to God's only way of eternal life—through Jesus Christ our Lord.

## Radical Islam and the Future

So, what is the future of radical Islam? I admit that the words *Islam* and *ISIS* do not appear in the Bible. Moses wouldn't have understood that any more than he would have understood a jetliner or a smartphone. But as we look at what Scripture says about the end times, I believe we see three mentions of what we know as radical Islam in God's prophetic future.

## The Islamic Invasion of Israel

First of all, Ezekiel 38:1–6 describes an Islamic invasion of Israel, led by Iran ("Persia" in verse 5) and other Muslim nations.[5] There is nothing in history that corresponds to this event; it hasn't happened yet. The *Moody Bible Commentary* makes this important observation: "All of the countries mentioned here by Ezekiel are today Muslim countries. Assuming their spiritual allegiance does not change, the future invasion of Israel by these nations will not be a Russian invasion, but an Islamic invasion. The coordination of attack on Israel will not come from Moscow, but from the leadership of these Muslim governments."[6]

The nations listed by Ezekiel in this future invasion are predominantly Muslim nations today. I believe that this is a group of Muslim nations that will attempt to invade Israel sometime during the tribulation. Interestingly, they will be defeated. God will intervene in that situation. He will deliver Israel out of Muslim hands, and there will two results of that deliverance.

The first result is that the nations will know that God has delivered Israel. In Ezekiel 39:21, God said, "I will set My glory among the nations; and all the nations will see My judgment which I have executed and My hand which I have laid on them." Remember, during the tribulation, God is giving the world one last chance to repent. And by His deliverance of Israel, He will prove to the nations that He really is God.

The second result will be that Israel will know God's power and faithfulness. Up to this point in the tribulation, Israel will not yet have known the Lord in true saving faith. God is trying to woo Israel to Himself. And as a result of this great act of deliverance, Ezekiel 39:22 says, "the house of Israel will know that I am the LORD their God from that day onward."

## The Army from the East

The second reference to radical Islam in Bible prophecy is the army from the east mentioned in Revelation 9 and 16. The Bible says in the final days, before Jesus returns, there will be a great battle on the plain of Megiddo. And leading up to that great battle, a massive army will march from the east. Revelation 9:16 describes the size of this army: "The number of the armies of the horsemen was two hundred million." And Revelation 16:12 describes their route: "The sixth angel poured out his bowl on the great river, the Euphrates; and its water was dried up, so that the way would be prepared for the kings from the east."

People used to read these verses and think, *This description can't be literal. What nation in the world could have an army that large?* But today, according to the CIA Facebook, China has over 318 million people "fit for military service," and India has over 249 million people "fit for military service." If we add to that the approximate 98 million from various Muslim countries surrounding Israel, it is easy to see how an army of 200 million could march from the east to Israel. The Bible says that's going to happen.

## Beheadings

The third reference to radical Islam in Bible prophecy is one, frankly, I hadn't seen until recently, and it has to do with the beheadings we're seeing more and more frequently. Did you know the Bible predicts beheadings will become common in the last days? In Revelation 20:4, John said, "I saw thrones, and they sat on them, and judgment was given to them. And I saw the souls of *those who had been beheaded* because of their testimony of Jesus and because of the word of God, and those who had not worshiped the beast or his image, and had not received the mark on their forehead and on their hand; and they came to life and reigned with Christ for a thousand years."

The Bible says that during the tribulation, when the Antichrist rules the earth, if you want to buy or sell anything, you have to take the mark of the beast.

Those who refuse to take the mark of the beast will be seen as disloyal to the Antichrist, and they will be executed—but not by a lethal injection, electric chair, or firing squad. They will be beheaded.

I used to read this passage and think, *Beheaded? That's an ancient practice. Surely John got it wrong here. Who in the future would ever resort to this barbaric way of execution?* But today, I think we have the answer.

How does the rise of radical Islam affect our understanding of the last days? Remember, Jesus said in Matthew 24:6 that "wars and rumors of wars" will increase in intensity and frequency as we get closer to His return. I believe we will continue to see beheadings and even greater acts of brutality from Islamic groups and nations. But their reign of terror is not going to last forever. All the things we're seeing in the world today are simply setting the stage for the greatest event in human history—the return of our Lord Jesus Christ.[7]

## Appendix B

# More Answers about the End Times

## What Is the Rapture?

As we have seen, the next event on God's prophetic timeline is what theologians call the rapture of the church. This event will mark the end of our current church age and usher in Daniel's final week (Daniel 9:27)—the seven-year period known as the tribulation.

Paul outlined the details of the rapture in 1 Thessalonians 4, in which he wrote, "We do not want you to be uninformed, brethren, about those who are asleep, so that you will not grieve as do the rest who have no hope. For if we believe that Jesus died and rose again, even so God will bring with Him those who have fallen asleep in Jesus" (vv. 13–14). The term "asleep" here refers to the physical body of a Christian when he dies, awaiting his resurrection.

Paul continued, "We who are alive and remain until the coming of the Lord, will not precede those who have fallen asleep. For the Lord Himself will descend from heaven with a shout, with the voice of the archangel and with the trumpet of God, and the dead in Christ will rise first. Then we who are alive and remain will be caught up together with them in the clouds to meet the Lord in the air, and so we shall always be with the Lord" (vv. 15–18).

Notice the four ingredients of this impending event. First, Christ will descend from heaven. Paul said, "The Lord Himself will descend from heaven" (v. 16). At the rapture, the Lord Jesus Christ will appear to His followers "in the air" (v. 17). In verse 15, Paul described the rapture as "the coming of the Lord." The word translated "coming" is the Greek word *parousia,* which is also used in Matthew 24:27 to describe the second coming of Christ.

The second aspect of the rapture is the resurrection of the "dead in Christ." When we die, our spirits go immediately into the presence of God. But our bodies are left behind, just as the body of Christ remained in the tomb until that first Easter morning. However, our bodies will not remain in the grave forever. When the trumpet of God sounds at the rapture, "the dead in Christ will rise first" (1 Thessalonians 4:16). The graves will be opened, and the physical bodies of believers will rise toward heaven.

Third, Christians who are alive on earth at the time of the rapture will be suddenly "caught up together with them in the clouds to meet the Lord in the air" (v. 17). This means that there will be a generation of Christians who will never experience death. They will suddenly be removed from the earth, just as Enoch and Elijah in the Old Testament were transported to heaven without ever experiencing death (Genesis 5:24; 2 Kings 2:11).

The fourth essential ingredient of the rapture is explained in 1 Corinthians 15:50–55. In verse 50, Paul was saying, "Here's a simple fact of life; you can't enter heaven in your present bodies. That which is temporal cannot enter that which is eternal."

So what is the solution to this dilemma? Paul said that, at the rapture, our bodies will experience a radical transformation: "Behold, I tell you a mystery; we will not all sleep, but we will all be changed, in a moment, in the twinkling of an eye, at the last trumpet; for the trumpet will sound, and the dead will be raised imperishable, and we will be changed. For this perishable must put on the imperishable, and this mortal must put on immortality" (vv. 51–53)

As we saw in 1 Thessalonians 4, not all Christians will die ("sleep"). Those Christians who are alive at the rapture will not taste death; instead, they'll be snatched away into heaven. However, every Christian must experience a transformation of his mortal body into an immortal body. As Paul put it, "We will all be changed" (1 Corinthians 15:51). At the rapture, our bodies, as well as the bodies of those who have already died, will be instantly transformed into the type of body Jesus possessed after His resurrection.

# Why Didn't Jesus Talk about the Rapture?

Though Jesus taught about various end-times events, He never specifically mentioned the rapture of the church. Why not? It's certainly not because He didn't know about it. The reason Jesus didn't mention the rapture is the same reason He didn't mention the church.

The church was a mystery the Old Testament prophets didn't understand, a secret that Jesus kept to Himself during His ministry on earth. After Jesus ascended into heaven, the apostle Paul was given the assignment of revealing the mystery of the church— that God would temporarily set aside Israel to give the Gentiles like you and me a chance to come to faith in Christ. Paul explained in Ephesians 3:2–6 that he was the steward of the "mystery" of the church.

That's why the apostle Paul is the one who talked about the rapture in the Bible. Since Paul was given the task of revealing the mystery of the church age (the period of time from Pentecost until the rapture), it makes sense that Paul was also the one who detailed the event that will signal the end of the church age—the rapture of the church.

# When Will the Rapture Occur?

As we have discussed in this book, the rapture is the next event on God's prophetic timeline. There are *no* prophecies that must be fulfilled prior to the rapture. In 1 Corinthians 15:52, Paul wrote, "In a moment, in the twinkling of an eye, at the last trumpet; for the trumpet will sound, and the dead will be raised imperishable, and we will be changed."

You and I should live every day with the realization that at any time, "in the twinkling of an eye," the trumpet could sound, the clouds could part, and the Lord could appear to snatch us away to be with Him in heaven.

# Who Will Be Raptured?

Only those who have placed their faith in Jesus Christ for the forgiveness of their sins during the church age will be included in the rapture of the church. Some scholars believe that all believers from all of history will be resurrected at the rapture. This would include all the Old Testament saints like Adam,

Noah, Abraham, Rahab, David, and Esther. However, I believe that only Christians who have been saved during the church age will be included in the rapture. The rapture is an event for the church. Other faithful believers—both those who lived before and and those who lived after Christ—will be resurrected to eternal life at other times.

## Where Will Christians Go When They Are Raptured?

Once we are raptured, we will go to the same place we would have gone if we had died before the rapture: the presence of God. We will worship Him along with all His holy angels. The only difference will be that we will also receive our resurrection bodies at that time.

Where, exactly, is the presence of God? It is in heaven—more specifically, in what is sometimes called the "third" heaven. The first heaven is Earth's atmosphere. The second heaven is outer space. The third heaven, the place where Christians go when we die, is the presence of God. The book of Revelation also describes a future, fourth heaven—called "the new heaven and new earth"—where we'll live for the rest of eternity.

In Revelation 4–5, the apostle John gave us a breathtaking picture of the present, third heaven.

In Revelation 4, John described the scene in heaven right after the church has been raptured. Then in Revelation 5, he revealed how the residents of heaven were praising God (vv. 9–10). How do I know these worshipers, called the "elders," represent the church in heaven? They say in verse 9, "You . . . purchased for God with Your blood men from every tribe and tongue and people and nation." Who are the people Jesus purchased with His blood? They're not angels. Angels were never redeemed; only the church has been redeemed.

And notice that these men and women who were purchased with Jesus's blood are "from every tribe and tongue and people and nation." The elders in heaven say that God has made the church "to be a kingdom and priests to our God; and they will reign upon the earth" (v. 10). This verse is talking about the privileges that await you and me as God's redeemed. The church is a royal family. We are coregents with God. This is proof that the elders represent the church, and they're in heaven in Revelation 5, which takes place after the rapture.

# What Happens to Christians Who Die before the Rapture?

Until the new heaven and the new earth are completed,

all Christians who die are immediately transported into the presence of God in the present, third heaven. They are very much alive and aware of their surroundings. The apostle Paul said, "Being always of good courage, and knowing that while we are at home in the body we are absent from the Lord—for we walk by faith, not by sight—we are of good courage, I say, and prefer rather to be absent from the body and to be at home with the Lord" (2 Corinthians 5:6–8).

This third heaven is the same place as "Paradise" (Luke 23:43; 2 Corinthians 12:2–4) and "Abraham's bosom" (Luke 16:22). The third heaven is not a state of mind. It's a very real location. But it's a temporary location; it's not our final home. The final home for all believers—once we are all resurrected—is the new heaven and new earth, which God has not completed yet. We humans were created to live forever, in physical bodies, on a physical planet, and we will inhabit the perfect new earth, where righteousness dwells.

# Where Did Old Testament Believers Go When They Died?

Where did Old Testament believers who lived before Christ go when they died? First, we need to understand that all believers, whether they lived before Christ or after Christ, are saved the same way: by faith in the death and resurrection of Jesus Christ. Those who lived before Christ were saved by placing their faith in God and in His promise to send a Messiah to save the world (Genesis 3:15). They did not know the name of Jesus yet, but they had enough information to be saved. For them, Christ's payment for their sin was credited to their account the moment they exercised faith in God's revelation. Abraham lived thousands of years before Christ, yet Genesis 15:6 says "he believed in the LORD; and He reckoned it to him as righteousness."

Second, it's important to understand two important biblical terms that refer to the place of the dead: the Hebrew word *sheol* and the Greek word *hades*. Both words mean roughly the same thing: "covered" or "hidden." Some scholars say that *sheol* is a holding place for the dead that is divided into two compartments: paradise (or "Abraham's bosom") is where the righteous reside, and *hades* is the place of torment where the unrighteous reside. They point to the beggar Lazarus in Jesus's story in Luke 16:19–31. Jesus said that after having been carried away by angels to "Abraham's bosom," Lazarus found comfort, blessing, and fellowship with the Old Testament patriarch.

Additionally, the weight of Scripture supports the interpretation that Abraham's bosom is the present (third) heaven. For example, it is implied that faithful Enoch was transported directly to heaven, and not to a holding place, when God "took him" (Genesis 5:24). Furthermore, 2 Kings 2:1 and 2:11 say that Elijah was taken "by a whirlwind to heaven." Moreover, David believed God would not "abandon [his] soul to Sheol," but would give him "fullness of joy" in God's presence (Psalm 16:10–11). David also rejoiced that after "all the days of [his life]," he would "dwell in the house of the LORD forever" (23:6). That can only refer to one place: heaven. Finally, David's son Solomon observed in Ecclesiastes 12:7, "The dust will return to earth as it was, and the spirit will return to God who gave it." In other words, Old Testament believers' bodies would decay and return as dust to the earth, but their spirits would continue to live in the presence of God. The evidence points to this being the same place as the present, third heaven. This is where believers who lived and died before Christ went—and where they are currently awaiting their resurrection.

# What Is the Purpose of the Tribulation?

To understand the purpose of the tribulation, we need to look at the visions God gave to Daniel in the sixth century BC while the Jews were captives in Babylon.

Daniel and the other exiles wanted to know:

- "Has God forgotten the promise He made to our father Abraham?"

- "Will we ever return to our homeland?"

- "Where is Israel's promised Deliverer when we need Him most?"

In response to their questions, God said through the angel Gabriel, "Seventy weeks have been decreed for your people and your holy city, to finish the transgression, to make an end of sin, to make atonement for iniquity, to bring in everlasting righteousness, to seal up vision and prophecy and to anoint the most holy place" (Daniel 9:24).

In that prophecy, Gabriel announced to Daniel that God will use 490 years to accomplish six goals:

1. *"To finish the transgression."* This is most likely a reference to the end of Israel's rebellion and unbelief.

2. *"To make an end of sin."* This phrase probably refers to an end to the sacrificial system.

3. *"To make atonement for iniquity."* I believe this phrase refers to the sacrificial death of

the Messiah, which provided the ultimate atonement (meaning "covering") for our sin.

4. *"To bring in everlasting righteousness."* This phrase refers to the establishment of the Messiah's rule over the earth, as prophesied in Isaiah 11.

5. *"To seal up vision and prophecy."* Once the Messiah's rule is established on earth, there will no longer be a need for prophecy (or for books on prophecy!).

6. *"To anoint the most holy place."* This refers to the temple in Jerusalem, which had been destroyed during the Babylonian invasion. This phrase anticipates a rebuilding of the temple and a re-establishment of the sacrificial system.

God has already accomplished goal 3—atoning for sin. Goals 1, 2, 4, 5, and 6 are all still to be fulfilled. God will use the tribulation to accomplish goal 1, bringing Israel to repentance and faith in Jesus as their prophesied Messiah. Jesus will then return and accomplish goals 4 and 5 at the end of the tribulation. But what about goals 2 and 6?

Zerubbabel rebuilt the temple in 516 BC, after

Israel's return from Babylon. That temple, however, after being enlarged by King Herod, was destroyed by the Romans in AD 70. During the first half of the coming seven-year tribulation, the Bible says that Israel will once again be offering sacrifices, which means the temple in Jerusalem is going to be rebuilt. Furthermore, sacrifices will be offered during Christ's thousand-year reign from David's throne in Jerusalem, known as the millennium, requiring yet another temple. So it appears that goals 2 and 6 are still future.

Let's look back to goal 1. How will God bring Israel to repentance? Gabriel provided the answer: "He [the world dictator known as the Antichrist] will make a firm covenant with the many for one week, but in the middle of the week he will put a stop to sacrifice and grain offering; and on the wing of abominations will come one who makes desolate, even until a complete destruction, one that is decreed, is poured out on the one who makes desolate" (Daniel 9:27).

This seven-year period of time during which God deals with the nation of Israel, as well as the unbelieving world, is known by a variety of titles: "the time of Jacob's distress," "Daniel's seventieth week," or "the tribulation."

But the most common biblical name for this seven-year period is "the day of the Lord." After these seven years, God's judgment against Israel and the unbelieving world will culminate in Christ's return and rule over the earth (Joel 1:15; Amos 5:18, 20; Zephaniah 1:14–15; 1 Thessalonians 5:2–3).

The Bible says that terrible judgment will accompany the day of the Lord. But even in the midst of His judgment, we see God's love. If God were simply interested in annihilating unbelievers, then why would He dispatch 144,000 evangelists to proclaim His message of salvation during the tribulation? Never forget that God's ultimate purpose during these final seven years is to bring Israel, as well as the rest of the world, to a saving relationship with Christ. As God said through the prophet Ezekiel, "I take no pleasure in the death of the wicked, but rather that the wicked turn from his way and live. Turn back, turn back from your evil ways! Why then will you die, O house of Israel?" (33:11).

What God desires for Israel and the world at large, He desires for you as well. The Creator of the universe so longs for a relationship with you that He'll use whatever means necessary to drive you into the arms of the one who loves you.

# What Makes the Tribulation Different from Other Times of Persecution?

Believers throughout history have endured times of testing. Jesus said, "In the world you have tribulation" (John 16:33). Jesus was not referring to the seven-year tribulation described in Revelation 6–19, but to the difficulties all Christians would face as a result of living in a sin-infected world.

Since Jesus spoke those words, believers in every age have experienced intense suffering for their faith. The writer of Hebrews described this persecution: "They were stoned, they were sawn in two, they were tempted, they were put to death with the sword; they went about in sheepskins, in goatskins, being destitute, afflicted, ill-treated (men of whom the world was not worthy), wandering in deserts and mountains and caves and holes in the ground" (11:37–38).

More than two thousand years after these words were written, followers of Jesus Christ are still being persecuted for their faith. More Christians died as martyrs during the twentieth century alone than in all other centuries combined. Christians are also subject to sickness, the breakdown of relationships, and the heartaches that come from living in a fallen world. But the kind of universal tribulation that all residents of the earth—believers and unbelievers—

experience is very different from the suffering that will characterize the final seven years of history known as the tribulation. The following are some ways that the future tribulation will be different from all other times of hardship:

- *Worldwide Wrath.* The distinguishing characteristic of the tribulation is that it's a time when God will pour out His wrath on an unbelieving world. Those living on the earth during this period of time will experience God's direct judgment for their disobedience in the form of seal, trumpet, and bowl judgments (Revelation 6; 8–9; and 16). This will be a time of trouble the world has never seen before, especially during the final three and a half years of the seven-year tribulation.

- *A Raptured Church.* God has promised to spare believers from the wrath He is bringing upon the earth. Paul assured the Roman Christians that "therefore there is now no condemnation for those who are in Christ Jesus" (Romans 8:1). Jesus will rapture His church from the earth before the tribulation.

- *A Universal Dictator.* I believe that the rapture of the church may coincide with some cataclysmic world event that will precipitate a universal clamor for a great leader to unite the nations. There have been many evil men throughout history who believed they were God and/or persecuted God's people, but never one who ruled the whole world (Daniel 9:27; Matthew 24:15–16, 29–30; Revelation 11:2; 13:5).

- *A One-World Government.* The Bible reveals that America and other freedom-loving countries will cease to exist before the world comes to an end! According to Daniel 7 and Revelation 17, during the tribulation, the Antichrist will preside over a ten-nation confederacy. This worldwide dictator will rise to power without a vote by the American people, and he will abrogate our most cherished freedoms, demanding that he alone be worshiped. Such a usurpation of power can only occur by the abolition of our Constitution. And once the Constitution is gone, the United States of America as we know it will cease to exist. All past persecutions have been local to some extent, but there will be no place on earth to escape the persecution during the tribulation (Daniel 7:21).

- *A Final False Prophet and False Religion.* Assisting the rise and rule of the Antichrist will be a man, empowered by Satan, whom the Bible refers to as the "false prophet." He will probably be a religious leader who will head a world church described as the "harlot" in Revelation. This apostate church will have the appearance of a legitimate church but will deny the basic tenets of Christianity. Throughout history, there have been many false prophets, false churches, and false religions. But during the tribulation, the false prophet will spread his false religion over the entire planet in service to the Antichrist.

- *The Mark of the Beast.* The false prophet will eventually control world commerce by limiting the purchase of goods to those who are willing to demonstrate their worship of the Antichrist by carrying the number 666 on their bodies (Revelation 13:16–18). In past persecutions, Christians and

Jews have sometimes been forced to wear distinctive identification. At other times, they have been banned from participating in commerce. But never before have both persecutions happened together, and never have they extended to every individual on earth as they will during the tribulation.

- *The Calling of 144,000 Witnesses.* Another important distinction of the tribulation will be the calling out of 144,000 witnesses from among the twelve tribes of Israel. These Jews who believe in Jesus Christ will preach the gospel over the whole earth (Revelation 7:5–8). Although the first Christians came from the nation of Israel, the majority of Jews throughout history have rejected their Messiah. This will change during the tribulation.

- *The Known Exact Duration.* Unlike all previous persecutions, we know exactly how long the tribulation will last: seven years. And we know that certain events will take place during the first three and a half years, at the midpoint, and during the second three and a half years (sometimes called the "great tribulation"). The tribulation will be severe, but it will also be completely in God's hands (Revelation 6–19).

# Will People Be Saved During the Tribulation?

Many people will be saved during the tribulation, and will be saved the same way you and I are saved: by grace through faith in Jesus Christ alone. But they will pay a steep price for their conversion. During the first three and a half years of the tribulation, God will call out 144,000 evangelists from the twelve tribes of Israel. These 144,000 witnesses will lead many Jews and Gentiles to Christ during the hardships of the tribulation. They will be supernaturally sealed and therefore protected by God from destruction by the Antichrist (Revelation 7:3–4).

It will happen this way: after the rapture of the church, 144,000 Jews will come to faith in Christ and will then start sharing the gospel with people from every nation, tongue, and tribe. Many people—both Jews and Gentiles—will choose to follow Christ during the tribulation, but Revelation 7:9, 14 says they will experience great persecution or even death for that choice.

I am often asked this question: "If it's still possible for people to be saved after the rapture, why not wait until then to see if all this stuff is really true?" The fact that many people will be saved after the rapture is no excuse for delaying your decision to trust in Christ. Think about it: If you're not willing to be saved during this age when many Christians (at least in America) are spared persecution, why would you be willing to be saved during the tribulation when you'll have to endure tremendous hardships for your faith? Nevertheless, during the tribulation, many people will come to faith in Jesus and risk their lives in defiance of the Antichrist in order to obtain eternal life.

# Who Is the Antichrist?

Although various people throughout history have had the attitude of the Antichrist (1 John 2:18), Scripture is clear that at the end, there will be one man, empowered by Satan, who takes this attitude to the extreme. He will oppose God's good purposes with every fiber of his being. Scripture calls him the "man of lawlessness," the "beast," the "little horn," or, most commonly, the "Antichrist." Let's look at passages describing him.

In Daniel 9:27, the angel Gabriel described the Antichrist's actions this way: "He will make a firm covenant with the many for one week, but in the middle of the week he will put a stop to sacrifice and grain offering; and on the wing of abominations will come one who makes desolate, even until a complete destruction, one that is decreed, is poured out on the one who makes desolate."

The final seven-year countdown known as the tribulation begins with this world dictator establishing a peace treaty with the nation of Israel. He will seem like a hero! However, halfway through those seven years, this ruler will betray Israel and instigate a period of unparalleled persecution against the people of God. These final three and a half years are often called the great tribulation (Matthew 24:21), a time that will climax with the return of Christ and the establishment of His kingdom.

Why would the nation of Israel sign a peace treaty with the Antichrist? I believe that the rapture of the church may coincide with some catastrophic world event that will cause many to clamor for a great leader to unite the nations. A disaster such as a nuclear accident, giant asteroid, financial meltdown, or another world war could be the catalyst that will set the stage for this world dictator. However, I think it's probable that a crisis in the Middle East will bring the Antichrist to the world stage.

It's easy to see how a future leader could win the respect of the world if he were able to establish what was perceived to be a lasting solution to the conflict in the Middle East, especially if that conflict had precipitated a worldwide economic crisis that would arise from any disruption of oil production.

By looking at several Bible passages, we discover several nteresting facts about the man known as the Antichrist. First, he will come to power after Christians are removed from the earth at the rapture, according to 2 Thessalonians 2:6–9 (although it's certainly possible that he could be alive today, since the rapture could occur at any time). Second, he most likely will be a Gentile. Revelation 13:1 describes him as coming out of the "sea" (a common biblical expression describing Gentiles, though it could also refer to the constant churning of the political world). Third, he will rule over a revived Roman Empire that will apparently be in the form of a ten-nation confederacy. Daniel 9:26–27 identifies those who kill the Messiah as "the people of the prince who is to come" and as the ones who destroyed the temple—a direct reference to the Romans who invaded Jerusalem and destroyed the temple in AD 70.

When I was in high school, I heard a rumor that President John F. Kennedy was still alive, living on a remote island in Greece, and was going to reemerge as the Antichrist. Proponents of this theory pointed to Revelation 13:3: "I saw one of his heads as if it had been slain, and his fatal wound was healed. And the whole earth was amazed and followed after the beast."

One explanation is that this verse is referring to a political resurrection of the beast's empire (Rome) rather than the physical resurrection of the Antichrist. The world will be amazed that the Roman Empire, thought to be dead, will be resurrected in the form of this ten-nation confederacy presided over by the Antichrist. That's one way to interpret this verse. But I believe John was describing an actual physical wound that will appear to be miraculously healed, causing people to follow the Antichrist.

Fourth, and perhaps most significant, the Antichrist will oppose the people of God and attempt to change the laws of God without opposition. This future world leader will launch unprecedented persecution against God's people, trying to "wear down the saints" (Daniel 7:25). Daniel also prophesied that the Antichrist would "intend to make alterations in times and in law" (v. 25).

It is significant that the Antichrist will be able to persecute God's people, seek to change God's laws, and usurp people's freedom of worship and commerce without any recorded opposition. How could that happen? The only explanation is that prior to the appearance of the Antichrist, people will have already become so numb to immorality, apathetic and even sympathetic to the persecution of religious "extremists" (which will be the new term for committed Christians), and conditioned to the government's usurpation of personal freedom, that the Antichrist's rise to power will go unchallenged.

# Who Is the False Prophet?

The Antichrist will not ascend to power on his own. Assisting his political rise will be a man, also empowered by Satan, commonly referred to as the "false prophet." As I mentioned earlier, the false prophet will probably be a religious leader who will lead the worldwide church described in Revelation 17–18 as the "harlot" and "Babylon." This false church will have the appearance of being legitimate, but it will deny the basic tenets of Christianity.

Some have tried to identify this false church as an already existing religious group or denomination. However, this future worldwide church most probably will be an amalgamation of various religious beliefs. Given our culture's increasing disdain for the absolute truth claims of historic Christianity, it's not hard to see how—in the name of world peace—a new syncretic religion could develop that is a mixture of some of the more appealing aspects of several world religions. Even today there are numerous churches that profess belief in the Bible, Jesus Christ, and the cross. And yet, when you peel away the religious trappings of these churches, you find a belief system that denies the essence of Christianity: that salvation is through faith alone in Christ's sacrificial death and resurrection.

During the first three and a half years of the seven-year tribulation, the false prophet will use his religious influence to promote the Antichrist's agenda. However, after those first three and a half years, the Antichrist will decide that he no longer needs this false church and will destroy it, directing all worship toward himself. John's vision in Revelation 17:16 depicted this event: "The [Antichrist] . . . will hate the harlot and will make her desolate and naked, and will eat her flesh and will burn her up with fire."

After the destruction of this apostate church, to further assist the Antichrist in achieving his goals, the false prophet will move from religion to the area he is really interested in: the economy. Specifically, the false prophet will control world commerce by limiting the purchase or sale of goods and services to those who are willing to demonstrate their allegiance to the Antichrist by carrying the mark of the beast. Revelation 13:16–18 says that the false prophet "causes all, the small and the great, and the rich and the poor, and the free men and the slaves, to be given a mark on their right hand or on their forehead, and he provides that no one will be able to buy or to sell, except the one who has the mark."

During the great tribulation, true believers are willing not to take the mark of the beast. They say no to food and comfort, and they say yes to martyrdom. Here's the irony: those who take the mark experience temporary comfort but end up in eternal torment, while those who stay obedient to Christ suffer temporary discomfort but are welcomed into eternity with Christ. Revelation 14:12 describes these tribulation believers: "Here is the perseverance of the saints who keep the commandments of God and their faith in Jesus." True saints of God, those who are truly saved, will stay true to the gospel and persevere until the end.

# What Happens to Unbelievers When They Die?

According to Jesus's story of the rich man and Lazarus in Luke 16, when unbelievers die, they are immediately dispatched to hades—a place of pain and agony.

Hades is the immediate, but temporary, destination of non-Christians when they die, just as the third heaven is the immediate, but temporary, destination of Christians who die. In the Old Testament, hades was called "sheol." Just as believers begin to immediately and consciously experience the comfort of being in God's presence as soon as they die, unbelievers begin to immediately experience the horrendous suffering of being separated from God at the moment of their death.

In Luke 16:26, Jesus said there's a "great chasm" between the righteous and unrighteous, preventing those in heaven from traveling to hades and those in hades from traveling to heaven, thereby eliminating any possibility of salvation after death.

In 2 Peter 2:9, Peter said, "The Lord knows how . . . to keep the unrighteous under punishment for the day of judgment." In this verse, "keep" is in the present tense, indicating that the wicked are held captive continuously in hades (or sheol), as a guard keeps careful watch over a condemned prisoner on death row. Once unbelievers die and are held for final judgment, their fate is fixed.

# What Does the Bible Mean When It Talks about Hell?

The New Testament uses three words to describe the destination of non-Christians. While all three of these words are translated as "hell" in many English versions of the Bible, the three Greek words denote different places.

First, the word *tartaros* (used only in 2 Peter 2:4) describes the place of judgment of the wicked angels described in Jude 6. Second, *gehenna* is used twelve times in the New Testament and primarily refers to the eternal lake of fire (Revelation 19:20; 20:10, 15) that will be the final residence of all unbelievers. The third word for hell is *hades*. It is used to describe the temporary location of the unsaved dead who are awaiting the great white throne judgment as described in Revelation 20:11–15.

This judgment is for unbelievers and is like the sentencing phase of a trial. At the end of the millennium, Jesus will resurrect all unbelievers from hades. Since these are all the people from the beginning of time who refused to accept Christ's righteousness on their behalf, they will stand or fall by their own righteousness. And the Bible is clear that we all fall far short of God's perfect standard. These rebellious unbelievers will be resurrected in bodies designed to endure the everlasting torments of the lake of fire (*gehenna*). They will stand before Jesus and receive their due punishment in the lake of fire. This is the final judgment, and it is only for unbelievers. The lake of fire is the eternal destination for all unbelievers, just as the new heaven and new earth is the eternal destination for all believers.

When we die, we immediately begin experiencing God's blessing or God's judgment. While it is true that at some future day believers will change location from the third heaven to the new heaven, and unbelievers will also change location from hades to the lake of fire, a change of location is not the same as a change of eternal destiny. Heaven and hell are eternal choices. If you wait until you die to choose your eternal destination, you'll have waited one second too long. Hell and heaven are forever choices.

## What Is the Difference between the Great White Throne Judgment and the Judgment Seat of Christ?

Contrary to what some people believe, there's not one final judgment that includes both believers and unbelievers. Instead, unbelievers will be judged separately from Christians at a judgment commonly referred to as the great white throne judgment.

### The Great White Throne Judgment

After Satan's final rebellion, God will cast him into the lake of fire for an eternity of punishment (Revelation 20:10). God will then destroy the present heaven and earth in preparation for the new heaven and earth (2 Peter 3:10; Revelation 20:11).

Prior to the tribulation, Revelation 4:2–5 pictures God sitting on a throne surrounded by a rainbow, flashes of lightning, and worshipers. But Revelation 20:11 describes a solitary throne suspended in space: "I saw a great white throne and Him who sat upon it, from whose presence earth and heaven fled away, and no place was found for them." This is obviously a different throne with a different occupant. Jesus Christ is seated on this throne as He prepares to judge those who have rejected Him. John continued, "And I saw the dead, the great and the small, standing before the throne. . . . And the sea gave up the dead which were in it, and death and Hades gave up the dead which were in them; and they were judged" (vv. 12–13).

By what standard will Christ judge the unbelievers who stand before Him at the great white throne judgment? It may surprise you to learn that unbelievers will be judged *by their works*. Revelation 20:12–13 says, "And books were opened; and another book was opened, which is the book of life; and the dead were judged from the things which were written in the books, *according to their deeds*. And the sea gave up the dead which were in it, and death and Hades gave up the dead which were in them; and they were judged, every one of them *according to their deeds.*"

God keeps two sets of books on each of us. First, there is the "book of life," which contains the name of every believer who has trusted in Christ. Revelation 13:8 and 17:8 explain that the name of every believer was entered into this book before the foundation of the world. Those whose names are written in this book of life have nothing to fear, but those whose names do not appear in the book of life have *everything* to fear: "And if anyone's name was not found written in the book of life, he was thrown into the lake of fire" (20:15).

God also keeps a second set of books that record all our deeds: the good, the bad, and the ugly. Every word, every thought, every action is carefully noted in our permanent record. This leads to the other judgment.

## The Judgment Seat of Christ

In Acts 18:8, we read that many "were believing and being baptized" in Corinth because of Paul's ministry. But many were also agitated by Paul's preaching, so they hauled him before the Roman proconsul Gallio to give an account for his actions: "But while Gallio was proconsul of Achaia, the Jews with one accord rose up against Paul and brought him before *the judgment seat*" (v. 12).

Paul later used this imagery of the judgment seat in reminding the Corinthian Christians of a coming evaluation of each of our lives: "Therefore we also have as our ambition, whether at home or absent, to be pleasing to Him. For we must all appear before *the judgment seat of Christ*, so that each one may be recompensed for his deeds in the body, according to what he has done, whether good or bad" (2 Corinthians 5:9–10).

Notice that Paul wrote "*We* must all appear," not "They must all appear." Paul is including himself in this future judgment that will be reserved for Christians. Every believer will one day answer to Christ for every thought, word, action, and motivation of his earthly life. But unlike the great white throne judgment, the purpose of this judgment is not condemnation but evaluation and commendation.

The judgment seat of Christ in no way invalidates the forgiveness we have received from Christ. When we trust in Jesus Christ as our Savior, we wrap ourselves in the righteousness of Christ. God no longer sees our sin; instead, He sees the perfection of His own Son. Nevertheless, the fact that we have been declared "not guilty" before God and are guaranteed a place in heaven does not negate the possibility of God's evaluation of our works.

Though our works are worthless to secure our *place* in heaven, they will play a large role in determining our *rank* in heaven. In Ephesians 2:8–10, the apostle Paul drew a distinction between works *before* salvation and works *after* salvation: "For by grace you have been saved through faith; and that not of yourselves, it is the gift of God; not as a result of works, so that no one may boast. For we are His workmanship, created in Christ Jesus *for* good works, which God prepared beforehand so that we would walk in them."

Think of a Christian's good works as building a house. When we become a Christian, we all have the same foundation for our lives: Jesus Christ. Nevertheless, we choose what kind of life we want to construct upon that foundation. Some choose to build palaces that will receive our heavenly Father's commendation. Others squander their time and resources and build grass huts that receive our Father's condemnation (1 Corinthians 3:11–15).

Not every Christian will experience the same degree of joy and satisfaction in eternity. Those who built their lives around trivial, earthly pursuits will experience measurable loss in the next life. Although their salvation is secure ("He himself will be saved," Paul said in 1 Corinthians 3:15), they will endure real and lasting regret as they see what could have been theirs had they invested their lives in building God's kingdom rather than their own. All Christians will feel overwhelming gratitude for escaping hell. But that gratitude will be tempered with a sense of loss as some believers realize what rewards might have been theirs in the new heaven and earth had they lived more faithfully for God.

# What Is the Difference between the Millennium and the New Heaven and Earth?

The millennial kingdom will involve a renovation of the present earth. But after those one thousand years are over, the present heavens and earth will be destroyed (2 Peter 3:7), and God will unveil His new heaven and earth. John described it this way: "I saw a new heaven and a new earth; for the first heaven and the first earth passed away, and there is no longer any sea. And I saw the holy city, new Jerusalem, coming down out of heaven from God, made ready as a bride adorned for her husband" (Revelation 21:1–2).

185

One way to understand the difference between the earth during the millennium and the new heaven and earth is to think of the words *renovate* and *re-create*. When I first came to be pastor of First Baptist Church Dallas, we decided to renovate our preschool and children's space with new carpet, paint, and some imaginative theming. Everyone was thrilled by the vast improvement. However, I also knew that this was only a temporary fix until we could accomplish our ultimate vision—the complete re-creation of our church campus that covered six blocks of downtown Dallas.

One Saturday morning, we imploded the entire campus (including the renovated children's area) with hundreds of pounds of dynamite, reducing the entire campus to a pile of rubble. After six months of removing the debris, we completely re-created our church, including building a brand-new, state-of-the-art children's facility. While the *renovated* children's space was vastly superior to what had been there for decades, it was nothing compared to the *re-created* facility our families are now enjoying.

In the same way, Christians during the millennium will be amazed at the improvement of the renovated earth under Christ's rule once He returns to end the tribulation and cast the Antichrist and false prophet into the lake of fire (Revelation 19:20).

At that point, part of the curse against the earth will be removed, the planet will enjoy a partial renovation, and Satan will be bound for a thousand years (one millennium). It's important to note that only Christians will enter the millennium; unbelievers are removed from the earth. Those believers who survive the tribulation will enter the millennium in their natural bodies, while those of us who return with Christ will be in our supernatural, resurrected bodies that we received at the rapture.

Although Christ will be ruling the world from David's throne in Jerusalem, He will delegate some of His ruling authority to the twelve apostles (Matthew 19:28), to the Christians martyred during the tribulation (Revelation 20:4), and to Christians who lived before the rapture (2 Timothy 2:12). We will assist Christ in ruling over cities, over other believers, and even over the angels (1 Corinthians 6:2–3).

At the end of the millennium, God will unleash Satan from the abyss and give him one last opportunity to deceive the world. In spite of the previous thousand years when Christ ruled the earth with perfect righteousness, John said that a multitude of people will choose to follow Satan and, as a result, will suffer God's judgment. Those who choose to follow Satan will be some of the children born during the millennial reign of Christ. Although these children will be the offspring of genuine believers (the descendants of Christians who survived the tribulation), they will have to make an individual choice to follow Christ. Such a choice is only possible if God releases Satan and provides them with an alternative. Amazingly, some of those who have enjoyed the millennial blessings of Christ's rule over the earth will nevertheless succumb to Satan's deception and join his final rebellion against God. Their choice to follow Satan should forever lay to rest the myth that a perfect environment guarantees right behavior.

After Satan's final rebellion, God will cast Satan into the lake of fire for an eternity of punishment (Revelation 20:10). God then destroys the present heavens and earth in preparation for the new heaven and earth (2 Peter 3:10–11; Revelation 20:11).

Why does God need to destroy the old heavens and old earth to create a new one? God created the existing heavens and earth as recorded in Genesis 1 and pronounced them "good." But sin spoiled all of that. Like leaving a classic 1955 Corvette to rot in the elements until it becomes a rust bucket, sin so corrupted our physical environment that God wants to create a better, newer model—one in which perfect righteousness dwells. Once He does this, God will have fulfilled His promise in Isaiah 65:17: "For behold, I create new heavens and a new earth; and the former things will not be remembered or come to mind."

Ultimately, we won't go up to heaven and leave this earth behind forever. Instead, God will bring the new heaven down to a newly created earth. In many ways, this new earth will resemble our present earth—but it will also be vastly improved.

This future heaven will be the place where all believers—Old Testament saints, New Testament saints, and all Christians from the time of Jesus's death and resurrection to date—will live for eternity. Furthermore, this new earth—like the old one—will be *physical* in nature (Revelation 21). Resurrected believers with new bodies—bodies like Jesus had after His resurrection—require a physical home. And God will create such a place for us—a physical place for our physically transformed bodies.

John also heard a voice saying, "[God] will wipe away every tear from their eyes; and there will no longer be any death; there will no longer be any mourning, or crying, or pain; the first things have passed away" (v. 4). The curse leveled against this present world (described in Genesis 3) will be fully lifted, and all of redeemed humankind will enjoy the world as God originally created it. Those who live on the new earth

189

will experience unbroken fellowship with God and one another in joyous, loving relationships untainted by sin.

# What Will Our Resurrected Bodies Be Like?

Scripture promises that our resurrection bodies will be like Jesus's resurrection body. John wrote, "We know that when He appears, *we will be like Him*, because we will see Him just as He is" (1 John 3:2).

In Colossians 1:18, Paul referred to Jesus's resurrection as "the firstborn from the dead." The word translated "firstborn" comes from the Greek word from which we get our English word *prototype*. Whenever a manufacturer builds a new automobile or airplane, they first build a prototype. Every other car or plane is then patterned after that first one. In the same way, Jesus's resurrection body was an example of what our bodies are going to be like.

In what specific ways will our new resurrection bodies be in "conformity with the body of His glory," as Paul promised in Philippians 3:21?

### Our Bodies Will Be Physical

In 1 Corinthians 15:39–50, Paul addressed the

question of what kind of resurrection bodies we will receive. The simple answer is that we'll have different bodies than the ones we now inhabit. Our heavenly bodies will differ from our earthly bodies.

Paul detailed the differences between our earthly and heavenly bodies: "It is sown a perishable body, it is raised an imperishable body; it is sown in dishonor, it is raised in glory; it is sown in weakness, it is raised in power; it is sown a natural body, it is raised a spiritual body. If there is a natural body, there is also a spiritual body" (vv. 42–44). The Greek word for "body" here is *soma*. In every instance in the New Testament, *soma* refers to a physical body. When Paul used *soma* in verse 44 in reference to the "natural body" and "spiritual body," he made it clear that our resurrection bodies will be just as physical as our natural bodies are.

To show His physicality, the resurrected Jesus shared a meal with His disciples. But even before His death and resurrection, Jesus promised His disciples they would gather at His banquet table and feast with Him during the millennial kingdom (Luke 22:29–30). This event during the millennium occurs after Jesus's and the disciples' resurrections, when they are living in their new bodies. This promise indicates that we, too, will share meals with Jesus and the disciples in our new bodies.

We will wear clothes in heaven. When John saw the resurrected Christ on Patmos, Jesus was "clothed in a robe reaching to the feet, and girded across His chest with a golden sash" (Revelation 1:13). And when Christ spoke to the church at Sardis, He told them, "He who overcomes will thus be clothed in white garments" (3:5).

We will also retain our sexual identities in heaven. Some have wrongly concluded that we'll be genderless in heaven because Paul claimed, "There is neither . . . male nor female . . . in Christ Jesus" (Galatians 3:28). But Paul wasn't referring to our gender in the next life. He was referring to our equality in Christ in this life. The fact that some people did not recognize the resurrected Lord immediately (like the two men on the road to Emmaus in Luke 24) strongly argues that Jesus looked like any other man instead of some otherworldly, sexless alien.

## Our Bodies Will Be Perfect

In heaven, "the first things [the things of the old earth] have passed away" (Revelation 21:4). Cancer, heart attacks, and strokes will all be things of the past. So will blindness, deafness, and paralysis, as well as gray hair, wrinkles, and widening girths. Missing limbs will be restored. From the top of our heads to the bottom of our feet, we'll be perfect in every way.

### Our Bodies Will Be Personal

Your body, your memories, your gifts and talents, and your passions are what make you *you*. In the resurrection, all these will be perfected and glorified, "in the twinkling of an eye" (1 Corinthians 15:52). But you won't become someone else or something else, such as an angel. You will become the *you* God intended you to be.

Consider this example: you probably have a computer and use certain software for word processing or developing spreadsheets. When an upgrade becomes available, you don't get a whole new program; you get a better version of the same program—only with new and better features. Likewise, with our resurrection, we'll have upgrades, including new features (though without the glitches or programming errors), but we'll still be who we are.

This was Jesus's point when He appeared to the disciples after the resurrection and said, "It is I Myself" (Luke 24:39). Who Jesus was before His death and resurrection is who He is after His death and resurrection. When we get to heaven, we will recognize each other as the unique individuals we are.

# What Will We Do in Heaven?

When God created Adam, He gave him two primary

responsibilities: to work and to worship (Genesis 2:8, 15; 3:8). Just as Adam had two primary responsibilities in Eden, we will have two primary responsibilities in the new heaven and earth.

First, *we will enjoy exhilarating worship like we've never experienced.* One of the most remarkable aspects of our worship in heaven will be seeing Jesus face-to-face. Our response to that experience will be unlike anything we've ever known on earth. Perhaps this insight might help you catch a glimpse of what our worship experience will be like in heaven.

We know the angelic host ceaselessly worships the Father and the Son with shouts of praise. According to John, the angels probably number in the hundreds of millions—"myriads of myriads, and thousands of thousands" (Revelation 5:11). The sound must be unlike anything heard on earth. Isaiah described the angelic worship of God taking place right now like this: "And the foundations of the thresholds [of the temple] trembled at the voice of [the angel] who called out [in worship to God]" (Isaiah 6:4).

One day we will add our voices to that ground-shaking heavenly chorus of angels, shouting "Hallelujah!"—praise be to our God. John said, "I looked, and behold, a great multitude which no one could count, from every nation and all tribes and peoples and tongues, standing before the throne and before the Lamb, clothed in white robes, and palm branches were in their hands; and they cry out with a loud voice, saying, 'Salvation to our God who sits on the throne, and to the Lamb'" (Revelation 7:9–10).

Worship in heaven will be spontaneous, genuine, and exhilarating. Rather than being a rare exception to the otherwise rote and programmed activity too many churchgoers engage in on most Sundays, this kind of worship will happen every time we are in God's presence in the new heaven and earth.

But in the new heaven and earth, worship will not be limited to formal times of praising God. Scripture tells us that worship is a continual awareness of, gratitude toward, and submission to God in everything we do (1 Corinthians 10:31). God is honored with my worship while I'm enjoying dinner with my daughters and thanking Him for them, sitting on a beach reflecting on His majestic power, or preparing for a difficult conversation and asking that I might reflect His point of view. We must quit thinking that we can only worship God while doing *nothing* else. Rather, we worship while doing *everything* else—including work.

Second, *in heaven we will have invigorating work that we enjoy.* God is a worker. He did not create the world and then retire (though He did take one day off). He worked before sin entered the world, and He continues to work while sin remains in the world. Jesus declared, "My Father is working until now, and I Myself am working" (John 5:17). Since we are created in the image of God, it should be no surprise that we have been created to work as well. Contrary to what many believe, work is not a curse from God as a result of Adam and Eve's sin in the garden. Before the first couple ever took a bite of the forbidden fruit, God gave them the responsibility of work: "Then the LORD God took the man and put him into the garden of Eden to cultivate it and keep it" (Genesis 2:15).

Although Eden was perfect, it was not self-sustaining. God created this slice of Paradise on earth, but He gave man the responsibility of cultivating it by tilling the soil and planting and harvesting crops. While it's true that Adam and Eve's work became much harder after the fall because of God's judgment, work has always been—and will always be—part of God's plan for each of us.

"Wait a minute, working for eternity?" you ask. "That sounds more like hell than heaven!" The only reason we wince at the concept of working for eternity is because our labor on earth has been burdened by the effects of sin's curse: bodies that grow tired, relationships that become strained, government regulations that are burdensome, and an environment that is uncooperative.

But in the new heaven and earth, all those effects will evaporate because "there will no longer be any curse" (Revelation 22:3). In this world, work—no matter how much we enjoy it—can be exhausting. In heaven, work will be nothing but exhilarating.

Obviously, once the curse of sin is removed from the earth, some jobs will automatically disappear. For example, there will be no need for doctors (disease will be eradicated), firefighters (destruction will be a thing of the past), or funeral directors (death will be eliminated). Even my job as a preacher will probably be eliminated, since there will be no sin to preach against and "the earth will be filled with the knowledge of the glory of the LORD" (Habakkuk 2:14).

Perhaps for us what was merely a hobby on earth will become a vocation in heaven. Or maybe God will assign us a new task—one we will be uniquely suited to perform. The majority of Christians should not be surprised that their work in the new heaven and earth may very well be an extension and enhancement of their work now—minus the impediments that currently drain the joy out of that work.[1]

# Notes

## Note from the Author

1. Jeff Diamant, "About Four-in-Ten U.S. Adults Believe Humanity is 'Living in the End Times,'" Pew Research Center, December 8, 2022, https://www.pewresearch.org/short-reads/2022/12/08/about-four-in-ten-u-s-adults-believe-humanity-is-living-in-the-end-times/.

2. Rachel Bowman, "Doomsday Prepping Goes Mainstream: 'Bug Out Bags' Fly off Shelves as a Third of Americans Admit to Buying Survival Kits amid Armageddon Fears," DailyMail.com, October 28, 2023, https://www.dailymail.co.uk/news/article-12646477/doomsday-prepping-bug-bags.html/.

3. Adapted from Robert Jeffress, *Clear Answers to Your Questions about the End Times* (Dallas: Pathway to Victory, 2019), 4–5.

## Introduction: Your Future Matters Today

1. Jim VandeHei and Mike Allen, "Behind the Curtain: Rattled U.S. Government Fears Wars Could Spread," Axios, October 20, 2023, https://www.axios.com/2023/10/20/biden-government-war-fears-israel-hamas.

2. Ibid.

3. Adapted from Robert Jeffress, *Rapture: Fact or Fantasy?* (Dallas: Pathway to Victory, 2020), 5–6; Jeffress, *Bible Prophecy Made Simple* (Dallas: Pathway to Victory, 2020).

## Chapter 1: What Does the Bible Mean by the End Times?

1. Hal Lindsey with Carole C. Carson, *The Late Great Planet Earth* (Grand Rapids: Zondervan, 1970).

2. Rachel Cole, "10 Failed Doomsday Predictions," *Encyclopaedia Britannica Online*, accessed November 20, 2019, http://www.britannica.com/list/10-failed-doomsday-predictions; R.C. Sproul, "Montanism," *Tabletalk Magazine*, January 23, 2009, http://tabletalkmagazine.com/daily-study/2009/01/montanism/.

3. Keith A. Mathison, "Y1K," *Tabletalk Magazine*, August 2010, http://tabletalkmagazine.com/article/2010/08/y1k/.

4. Geoffrey James, "14 Fools Who Predicted the End of the World," CBS News, October 28, 2011, http://www.cbsnews.com/media/14-fools-who-predicted-the-end-of-the-world/.

5. Valerie I. J. Flint, et al., "Christopher Columbus," *Encyclopaedia Britannica Online*, July 17, 2019, http://www.britannica.com/biography/Christopher-Columbus.

6. "William Miller: Mistaken Founder of Adventism," *Christianity Today*, accessed November 14, 2019, http://www.christianitytoday.com/history/people/denominationalfounders/william-miller.html.

7. Matt Slick, "Jehovah's Witnesses and Their Many False Prophecies," Christian Apologetics and Research Ministry, December 5, 2008, http://carm.org/jehovahs-witnesses-and-their-many-false-prophecies.

8. Robert McFadden, "Harold Camping, Dogged Forecaster of the End of the World, Dies at 92," *New York Times*, December 17, 2013, http://www.nytimes.com/2013/12/18/us/harold-camping-radio-entrepreneur-who-predicted-worlds-end-dies-at-92.html.

9. McFadden, "Harold Camping"; Rick Paulas, "What Happened to Doomsday Prophet Harold Camping After the World Didn't End?" *Vice Magazine*, November 6, 2014, http://www.vice.com/en_us/article/yvqkwb/life-after-doomsday-456.

10. Maxine Lott, "10 Times 'Experts' Predicted the World Would End by Now," Fox News, March 19, 2020, http://www.foxnews.com/science/10-times-experts-predicted-the-world-would-end-by-now.

11. Ibid.

12. Ibid.

13. Ibid.

14. William Cummings, "'The World Is Going to End in 12 Years If We Don't Address Climate Change,' Ocasio-Cortez says," *USA Today*, January 22, 2019, http://www.usatoday.com/story/news/politics/onpolitics/2019/01/22/ocasio-cortez-climate-change-alarm/2642481002/.

15. Clare Herbert, "How Long Is a Normal Pregnancy?," BabyCentre, July 2019, http://www.babycentre.co.uk/x25015771/how-long-is-a-normal-pregnancy.

16. Sarah Johnson, "What Causes Your Water to Break When You're Pregnant?," We Have Kids, April 17, 2018, http://wehavekids.com/having-baby/What-Causes-Your-Water-to-Break-When-Youre-Pregnant; Vilma Ruddock, "How Long After the Water Breaks Before the Baby Is Born?," Love to Know, accessed November 15, 2019, https://www.lovetoknow.com/parenting/pregnancy/how-long-after-water-breaks-before-baby-is-born. See also Heidi Murkoff, *What to Expect When You're Expecting* (New York: Workman, 2016), 372–459.

17. Adapted from Robert Jeffress, *Clear Answers to Your Questions about the End Times* (Dallas: Pathway to Victory, 2019), 7–9.

18. Adapted from Robert Jeffress, *Perfect Ending* (Brentwood, TN: Worthy, 2014), 83–85.

19. Content in this chapter adapted from Robert Jeffress, *The Rapture: Fact or Fantasy?* (Dallas: Pathway to Victory, 2020), 5–24

## Chapter 2: What Role Does Israel Play in the End Times?

1. Adapted from Robert Jeffress, opening remarks, First Baptist Dallas, October 8, 2023.

2. For more about the millennium and God's promise to believing Israel, see my book *Final Conquest: A Verse-by-Verse Study of the Book of Revelation* (Dallas: Pathway to Victory, 2020).

3. Hendrik van Loon, *The Story of Mankind* (New York: Boni & Liveright, 1921), 2.

4. Content in this chapter adapted from Robert Jeffress, *Walking by Faith: A Study of the Life of Abraham* (Dallas: Pathway to Victory, 2023), 5–18; Jeffress, "It Begins and End with Israel," sermon, First Baptist Dallas, September 15, 2013.

## Chapter 3: What News Events Signal the End Times?

1. Karl Barth, as quoted in "Barth in Retirement," *Time*, May 31, 1963, http://content.time.com/time/subscriber/article/0,33009,896838,00.html.

2. Jamie Wilde, "The Occult Is Having a Moment," Morning Brew, October 29, 2021 https://www.morningbrew.com/daily/stories/2021/10/29/the-occult-is-having-a-moment.

3. Leon Trotsky, as quoted in Charles J. V. Murphy, "The Hazards of Being Late Too Often," *LIFE*, December 26, 1960, https://books.google.com/books?id=-1QEAAAAMBAJ.

4. According to the World Atlas, there are around 1.7 billion followers of Islam. If 5 percent of that number became radicalized, that would be eighty-five million people. See "How Many Muslims Are There in the World?" World Atlas, https://www.worldatlas.com/articles/how-many-muslims-in-the-world.html.

5. Content in this chapter adapted from Robert Jeffress, "The Beginning of the End?" sermon, First Baptist Dallas, April 19, 2015; Jeffress, "Jesus on the End Times," sermon, First Baptist Dallas, April 26, 2015; Jeffress, "Christians in the Crosshairs," sermon, First Baptist Dallas, May 10, 2015.

## Chapter 4: What Are the Major Events of the End Times?

1. For deeper teaching about Bible prophecy, see my books *Perfect Ending: Why Your Eternal Future Matters Today* (Nashville: Hachette, 2014); *Final Conquest: A Verse-by-Verse Study of the Book of Revelation*

(Dallas: *Pathway to Victory*, 2020); and *Mysteries of the End Times: 5 Little Known Truths about God's Plans for the Future* (Dallas: Pathway to Victory, 2023).

2. For more about what the Bible teaches about heaven, see my book *A Place Called Heaven: 10 Surprising Truths about Your Eternal Home* (Grand Rapids: Baker, 2017).

3. Content in this chapter adapted from Robert Jeffress, *What Every Christian Should Know: 10 Core Beliefs for Standing Strong in a Shifting World* (Grand Rapids: Baker, 2023), 201–22; Jeffress, *Bible Prophecy Made Simple* (Dallas: Pathway to Victory, 2020).

## Chapter 5: What Is the Difference between the Rapture and the Second Coming in the End Times?

1. Matthew Bridges, "Crown Him with Many Crowns" (1851), Hymnary.org, https://hymnary.org/text/crown_him_with_many_crowns.

2. Content in this chapter adapted from Robert Jeffress, *Clear Answers to Your Questions about the End Times* (Dallas: Pathway to Victory, 2019), 23–27; Jeffress, *The Rapture: Fact or Fantasy?* (Dallas: Pathway to Victory, 2020), 25–57; Jeffress, *Final Conquest: A Verse-by-Verse Study of the Book of Revelation* (Dallas: Pathway to Victory, 2020), 272–84.

## Chapter 6: Why Has God Delayed the End Times?

1. All Israel News Staff, "Judgment and Rapture Coming Soon, Daughter of Billy Graham Tells the Rosenberg Report," All Israel News, June 21, 2023, https://allisrael.com/judgment-and-rapture-coming-soon-daughter-of-billy-graham-tells-the-rosenberg-report.

2. Content in this chapter adapted from Robert Jeffress, *Clear Answers to Your Questions about the End Times* (Dallas: Pathway to Victory, 2019), 14–18; Jeffress, "How Should We Now Live?" sermon, First Baptist Dallas, May 24, 2015.

## Chapter 7: How Do I Prepare for the End Times?

1. Billy Graham, *World Aflame* (Billy Graham Evangelistic Association, 1965).

2. Story attributed to Billy Graham in Robert Jeffress, *Countdown to the Apocalypse: Why ISIS and Ebola Are Only the Beginning* (Nashville: FaithWords, 2015), 105.

3. David A. Graham, "Defense Secretary Chuck Hagel: Get Used to Endless War," *The Atlantic*, October 29, 2014, http://www.theatlantic. com/international/archive/2014/10/defense-secretary-chuck-hagel-get-used-to-endless-war/382079/.

4. Richard John Neuhaus, as quoted in David Neff, "Why Hope Is a Virtue," *Christianity Today*, April 3, 1995, 24.

5. A. W. Tozer, *This World: Playground or Battleground?* (Chicago: Moody, 1989), chap. 2, Kindle.

6. Content in this chapter adapted from Robert Jeffress, *Clear Answers to Your Questions about the End Times* (Dallas: Pathway to Victory, 2019), 95–96; Jeffress, *The Rapture: Fact or Fantasy?* (Dallas: Pathway to Victory, 2020), 95–125; Jeffress, "How Should We Now Live?" sermon, First Baptist Dallas, May 24, 2015.

## Appendix A: The Rise of Radical Islam

1. Interview with Robert Spencer on "Today's Issues," American Family Radio, October 8, 2014.

2. "How Many Muslims Are There in the World?" World Atlas, https://www.worldatlas.com/articles/how-many-muslims-in-the-world.html.

3. "In Assembly Speech, Israel's Netanyahu Warns against 'Militant Islam'; Denounces UN Rights Council," UN News, September 29, 2014, https://news.un.org/en/story/2014/09/479772/.

4. *The Nelson Study Bible*, Earl D. Radmacher, gen. ed. (Nashville: Thomas Nelson, 1997), 34.

5.   For more about this future invasion of Iran, see "The Mystery of Gog and Magog" in my book *Mysteries of the End Times* (Dallas, Pathway to Victory, 2023), 73–89.

6.   *Moody Bible Commentary* (Chicago: Moody, 2014), loc. 52451–52454, Kindle.

7.   Content adapted from Robert Jeffress, "The Rise of Radical Islam," sermon, First Baptist Dallas, May 3, 2015.

## Appendix B: More Answers about the End Times

1.   Content adapted from Robert Jeffress, *Clear Answers to Your Questions about the End Times* (Dallas: Pathway to Victory, 2019); Jeffress, *The Rapture: Fact or Fantasy?* (Dallas: Pathway to Victory, 2020), 127–58.

# About Dr. Robert Jeffress

Dr. Robert Jeffress is senior pastor of the sixteen-thousand-member First Baptist Church in Dallas, Texas, and a Fox News contributor. He has made more than four thousand guest appearances on various radio and television programs and regularly appears on major mainstream media outlets such as Fox News Channel's *Fox & Friends*, *Hannity*, *Fox News @ Night*, and *Varney & Co.*, as well as HBO's *Real Time with Bill Maher*.

Established in 1996, *Pathway to Victory* serves as the broadcast ministry of Dr. Jeffress and exists to pierce the darkness with the light of God's Word through the most effective media available. The daily radio program airs on more than one thousand stations. The daily television program can be seen Monday through Friday and every Sunday on more than eleven thousand cable and satellite systems, including the Trinity Broadcasting Network, where it has been the #1 viewed program since 2020. *Pathway to Victory* broadcasts reach all major markets in the United States plus 195 countries throughout the world. Additionally, *Pathway to Victory* ministers globally through podcasting and social and digital media. On each daily broadcast, Dr. Jeffress provides practical application of God's Word to everyday life through clear, uncompromised biblical teaching.

Dr. Jeffress is the author of more than thirty books, including *Perfect Ending*, *Not All Roads Lead to Heaven*, *A Place Called Heaven*, *Choosing the Extraordinary Life*, *Courageous*, *Invincible*, *18 Minutes with Jesus*, and *What Every Christian Should Know*.

Dr. Jeffress graduated with a DMin from Southwestern Baptist Theological Seminary, a ThM from Dallas Theological Seminary, and a BS from Baylor University. In May 2010, he was awarded a Doctor of Divinity degree from Dallas Baptist University. In June 2011, Dr. Jeffress received the Distinguished Alumnus of the Year award from Southwestern Baptist Theological Seminary. He is also an adjunct professor at Dallas Theological Seminary.

Dr. Jeffress and his wife, Amy, have two daughters and three grandchildren.

# About *Pathway to Victory*

Established in 1996, *Pathway to Victory* serves as the broadcast ministry of Dr. Robert Jeffress.

*Pathway to Victory* stands for truth and exists to pierce the darkness with the light of God's Word through the most effective media available, including television, radio, print, and digital media.

Through *Pathway to Victory*, Dr. Jeffress spreads the good news of Jesus Christ to a lost and hurting people, confronts an ungodly culture with God's truth, and equips the saints to apply Scripture to their everyday lives. More than one thousand radio stations in the United States broadcast the daily radio program, while Daystar, Trinity Broadcasting Network, and other Christian television networks air *Pathway to Victory* both in the United States and internationally.

Our mission is to provide practical application of God's Word to everyday life through clear, biblical teaching. Our goal is to lead people to become obedient and reproducing disciples of Jesus Christ, as He commanded in Matthew 28:18–20. As our ministry continues to grow and expand, we are confident the Lord will use *Pathway to Victory* to to transform the world with God's Word . . . one life at a time.